SCHOLASTIC

BOOK
OF
WORLD
RECORDS
2012

by Jenifer Corr Morse

A Georgian Bay Book

SCHOLASTIC INC.

NEW YORK • TORONTO • LONDON • AUCKLAND
SYDNEY • MEXICO CITY • NEW DELHI • HONG KONG

To Isabelle Nicole—May you always find wonder in the world.
—JCM

CREATED AND PRODUCED BY GEORGIAN BAY LLC
Copyright © 2011 by Georgian Bay LLC

GEORGIAN BAY STAFF
Bruce S. Glassman, Executive Editor
Jenifer Corr Morse, Author
Amy Stirnkorb, Designer

ISBN 978-0-545-33149-4

10 9 8 7 6 5 4 3   12 13 14 15

Printed in the U.S.A.   40
First edition, November 2011

In most cases, the graphs in this book represent the top five record holders in each category. However, in some graphs, we have chosen to list well-known or common people, places, animals, or things that will help you better understand how extraordinary the record holder is. These may not be the top five in the category. Additionally, some graphs have fewer than five entries because so few people or objects reflect the necessary criteria.

Due to the publication date, the majority of statistics is current as of May 2011.

contents

POP CULTURE. **5**
Television. 6
Movies. 15
Music. 34
Theater 49

SPORTS **51**
Basketball 52
Football. 62
Bicycling 71
Golf. 72
Baseball. 76
Track & Field .89
Tennis. 90
Olympics 94
Soccer. 99
Car Racing 103
Motorcycling. 107
Horse Racing 109
Hockey. 110
X Games. 114
Snowboarding. 116

SCIENCE. **117**
Video Games. 118
Internet. 121
Technology. 128
Vehicles. 132

NATURE **144**
  Natural Formations 145
  Animals 153
  Weather 191
  Plants 197
  Disasters 203
  Environment 209

MONEY **210**
  Most Expensive 211
  Most Valuable 218
  Big Business 220

HUMAN-MADE **224**
  Structures 225
  Travel 234
  Transportation 241
  Cities 244

US **245**

INDEX **296**
PHOTO CREDITS **303**
BONUS SECTION **305**
READ FOR THE WORLD RECORD **318**
THE MALAYSIA BOOK OF RECORDS **320**

pop culture records

television • movies • music • theater

highest-paid tv actor

Charlie Sheen

Before he was fired, Charlie Sheen got $1.25 million an episode for his role as Charlie Harper on the hit CBS sitcom *Two and a Half Men*, which he also helped produce. The Emmy-winning show was consistently one of the top-rated comedies each year. For this role, Sheen had been nominated for two Golden Globe Awards and four Emmy Awards. Before Sheen graced the TV screen, he appeared in many successful movies, including *Platoon* (1986), *Major League* (1989), *Hot Shots!* (1991), and *Scary Movie 3* (2003). Sheen got his star on the Hollywood Walk of Fame in 1994.

highest-paid tv actors

money earned per episode during the 2010–2011 season, in US dollars

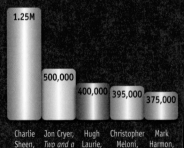

Charlie Sheen, Two and a Half Men	Jon Cryer, Two and a Half Men	Hugh Laurie, House	Christopher Meloni, Law & Order: SVU	Mark Harmon, NCIS
1.25M	500,000	400,000	395,000	375,000

highest-paid tv actresses

The Desperate Housewives

Marcia Cross, Teri Hatcher, Felicity Huffman, and Eva Longoria Parker—the main cast of the hit show *Desperate Housewives*—each make $440,000 an episode. The ladies of Wisteria Lane are better known as Bree Hodge (Cross), Susan Mayer (Hatcher), Lynette Scavo (Huffman), and Gabrielle Solis (Longoria Parker) to television audiences. Executive producer Marc Cherry brought this nighttime soap to life in 2004, and since then the show has won seven Emmy Awards and three Golden Globes.

highest-paid tv actresses

money earned per episode during the 2010–2011 season, in US dollars

440,000	440,000	440,000	440,000	395,000
Marcia Cross, *Desperate Housewives*	Teri Hatcher, *Desperate Housewives*	Felicity Huffman, *Desperate Housewives*	Eva Longoria Parker, *Desperate Housewives*	Mariska Hargitay, *Law & Order: SVU*

television

Angus T. Jones

Seventeen-year-old Angus T. Jones earns a hefty $300,000 per episode for his role as Jake Harper on *Two and a Half Men*. Over the next two seasons, Jones will earn a total of $7.8 million—plus a $500,000 signing bonus. The sitcom, which also stars Jon Cryer, has been among the top 20 most-watched programs since it first aired in 2003. Jones has also appeared in several movies, including *See Spot Run, The Rookie, Bringing Down the House*, and *George of the Jungle 2*. When he's not in front of a camera, he volunteers for organizations such as Big Brothers Big Sisters and St. Jude's Children's Research Hospital.

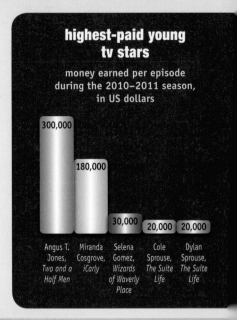

highest-paid young tv stars

money earned per episode during the 2010–2011 season, in US dollars

Angus T. Jones, *Two and a Half Men*	Miranda Cosgrove, *iCarly*	Selena Gomez, *Wizards of Waverly Place*	Cole Sprouse, *The Suite Life*	Dylan Sprouse, *The Suite Life*
300,000	180,000	30,000	20,000	20,000

top-earning reality star

Kim Kardashian

Reality TV star Kim Kardashian earned a very real $6 million in 2010. Kardashian stars alongside her sisters Kourtney and Khloe in the reality show *Keeping Up with the Kardashians*. The trio also wrote an autobiography and have recently launched a new clothing line at Sears. Kardashian has some other successful projects of her own. She has created several fragrances and a DVD workout series. Kardashian also competed on *Dancing with the Stars* in 2008, and appeared in guest spots on *How I Met Your Mother* in 2009 and *90210* in 2010.

top-earning reality stars

earnings in 2010, in millions of US dollars

Kim Kardashian	Lauren Conrad	Bethenny Frankel	Audrina Patridge	Kate Gosselin
6.0	5.0	4.0	3.5	3.5

television

tv show with the most Emmy awards

Frasier

Frasier—a hugely popular show that ran between 1993 and 2004—picked up 37 Emmy Awards during its 11 seasons. The sitcom focused on the life and family of psychiatrist Dr. Frasier Crane, played by Kelsey Grammer. His costars included David Hyde Pierce, John Mahoney, Peri Gilpin, and Jane Leeves. Some of the 37 awards the series won include Outstanding Comedy Series, Lead Actor in a Comedy Series, Supporting Actor in a Comedy Series, Directing in a Comedy Series, Editing, and Art Direction.

tv shows with the most Emmy awards

emmys won

37	29	28	26	25
Frasier	The Mary Tyler Moore Show	Cheers	Hill Street Blues	The Carol Burnett Show

The Daily Show with Jon Stewart & The Amazing Race

Two television shows—*The Daily Show with Jon Stewart* and *The Amazing Race*—are tied for the most consecutive Emmy wins with seven each. Comedy Central's *The Daily Show* is a fake news program and has been hosted by Jon Stewart since 1999. The show picked up Emmys for Outstanding Variety, Music, or Comedy Series, and Outstanding Writing for Outstanding Variety, Music or Comedy Program. *The Amazing Race* on CBS has won the Emmy for Outstanding Reality Competition Program since the award was first given in 2003. The show is hosted by Phil Keoghan and produced by Jerry Bruckheimer.

tv shows with the most consecutive Emmy awards

emmys won

The Daily Show with Jon Stewart, 2003–2009	The Amazing Race, 2003–2009	Frasier, 1994–1998	The Late Show with David Letterman, 1998–2002	The West Wing, 2000–2003
7	7	5	5	4

television

Jon Stewart

most popular scripted tv show

NCIS

Crime drama *NCIS* averages more than 20 million viewers each week. The show, which stands for Naval Criminal Investigation Service, focuses on a team of agents that investigate crimes involving the Navy and Marine Corps. *NCIS* premiered in 2003 and stars Mark Harmon (Supervisory Special Agent Leroy Jethro Gibbs), Michael Weatherly (Agent Anthony DiNozzo), Sean Murray (Agent Tim McGee), and Cote De Pablo (Agent Ziva David). The show has been nominated for several Emmy and People's Choice awards, and won six ASCAP Awards.

most popular scripted tv shows

viewers per week, in millions

NCIS	NCIS: Los Angeles	The Mentalist	Two and a Half Men	Criminal Minds
20.1	17.5	15.3	14.6	14.6

most popular reality tv show

American Idol

More than 7 percent of the TV-viewing audience tuned in during the 2010 season to watch the ninth installment of *American Idol*. During this ultimate reality singing contest, viewers watched Lee DeWyze defeat Crystal Bowersox after fans cast nearly 100 million votes—the most votes in *Idol* history. Dewyze bested 35 other contestants and braved comments from judges Simon Cowell, Ellen DeGeneres, Randy Jackson, and Kara DioGuardi. *American Idol* is one of just three television shows that have been rated number one for six consecutive seasons.

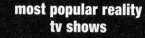

most popular reality tv shows

average audience percentage in 2010

American Idol	American Idol Results	Dancing with the Stars	Dancing with the Stars Results	Survivor: Heroes vs. Villains
7.9	7.5	7.1	5.5	4.3

television

Lee DeWyze

highest-paid talk show host

Oprah Winfrey

Oprah Winfrey pulled in $315 million in 2010, making her the world's highest-paid entertainer. In total, she is worth more than $1.5 billion. Winfrey's self-made millions have come mostly from her television show, which began in 1983. Since then, Winfrey has been educating her viewers and helping her audience with tough social issues. The megastar is also involved in movies, television production, magazines, books, radio, and the Internet. In January 2011, Oprah debuted her own channel called OWN: Oprah Winfrey Network. The network will include several talk and medical shows.

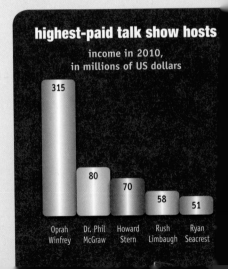

highest-paid talk show hosts

income in 2010,
in millions of US dollars

315				
	80	70	58	51
Oprah Winfrey	Dr. Phil McGraw	Howard Stern	Rush Limbaugh	Ryan Seacrest

Ben-Hur, Titanic, & The Lord of the Rings: The Return of the King

The only three films in Hollywood history to win 11 Academy Awards are *Ben-Hur*, *Titanic*, and *The Lord of the Rings: The Return of the King*. Some of the Oscar wins for *Ben-Hur*—a biblical epic based on an 1880 novel by General Lew Wallace—include Best Actor (Charlton Heston) and Director (William Wyler). Some of *Titanic*'s Oscars include Best Cinematography, Visual Effects, and Costume Design. *The Lord of the Rings: The Return of the King* is the final film in the epic trilogy based on the works of J. R. R. Tolkien. With 11 awards, it is the most successful movie in Academy Awards history because it won every category in which it was nominated. Some of these wins include Best Picture, Director (Peter Jackson), and Costume Design.

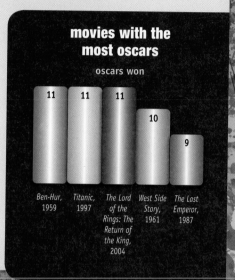

movies with the most oscars
oscars won

Ben-Hur, 1959	Titanic, 1997	The Lord of the Rings: The Return of the King, 2004	West Side Story, 1961	The Last Emperor, 1987
11	11	11	10	9

Presenters and the cast of *The Lord of the Rings* (Peter Jackson in front)

actress with the most oscar nominations

Meryl Streep

Meryl Streep is the most nominated actress in the history of the Academy Awards with 16 chances to win a statue. Her first nomination came in 1979 for *The Deer Hunter*, and was followed by *Kramer vs. Kramer* (1980), *The French Lieutenant's Woman* (1981), *Sophie's Choice* (1982), *Silkwood* (1983), *Out of Africa* (1985), *Ironweed* (1987), *A Cry in the Dark* (1988), *Postcards From the Edge* (1990), *The Bridges of Madison County* (1995), *One True Thing* (1998), *Music of the Heart* (1999), *Adaptation* (2002), *The Devil Wears Prada* (2006), *Doubt* (2008), and *Julie and Julia* (2009). Streep won her first Academy Award for *Kramer vs. Kramer*, and followed with a second win for *Sophie's Choice*.

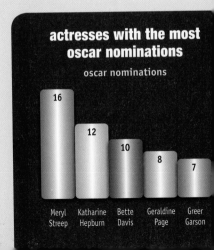

actresses with the most oscar nominations

oscar nominations

Meryl Streep	Katharine Hepburn	Bette Davis	Geraldine Page	Greer Garson
16	12	10	8	7

actor with the most oscar nominations
Jack Nicholson

Jack Nicholson has been nominated for a record 12 Oscars during his distinguished career. He is one of only three men to have been nominated for an acting Academy Award at least once every decade for five decades. He was nominated for eight Best Actor awards for his roles in *Five Easy Pieces* (1970), *The Last Detail* (1973), *Chinatown* (1974), *One Flew Over the Cuckoo's Nest* (1975), *Prizzi's Honor* (1985), *Ironweed* (1987), *As Good As It Gets* (1997), and *About Schmidt* (2002). He was nominated for Best Supporting Actor for *Easy Rider* (1969), *Reds* (1981), *Terms of Endearment* (1983), and *A Few Good Men* (1992). Nicholson picked up statues for *One Flew Over the Cuckoo's Nest*, *Terms of Endearment*, and *As Good As It Gets*.

actors with the most oscar nominations

oscar nominations

Jack Nicholson	Laurence Olivier	Paul Newman	Spencer Tracy	Al Pacino
12	10	9	9	8

actor with the most mtv movie awards

Jim Carrey

Jim Carrey has won 11 MTV Movie Awards since the television station began awarding them in 1992. He has won the award for Best Comedic Performance six times for his roles in *Dumb & Dumber* (1995), *Ace Ventura II: When Nature Calls* (1996), *The Cable Guy* (1997), *Liar Liar* (1998), *How the Grinch Stole Christmas* (2001), and *Yes Man* (2009). Carrey won the award for Best Male Performance twice for *Ace Ventura II: When Nature Calls* and *The Truman Show* (1999). He also won awards for Best Kiss for *Dumb & Dumber*, Best Villain for *The Cable Guy*, and the MTV Generation Award in 2006.

actors with the most mtv movie awards

awards won

Jim Carrey	Mike Myers	Adam Sandler	Robert Pattinson	Will Smith
11	7	6	5	5

Alicia Silverstone, Kristen Stewart, & Uma Thurman

Alicia Silverstone, Kristen Stewart, and Uma Thurman are tied for the most MTV Movie Awards with four statues apiece. Silverstone won her first two awards in 1994 for her movie *The Crush*. She picked up two more in 1996 for her role in *Clueless*. Stewart picked up her first two awards in 2008 for her role as Bella Swan in *Twilight*. The next year she picked up two more for the same role in *New Moon*. Thurman won an award in 1995 for *Pulp Fiction* and two more in 2004 for *Kill Bill: Volume 1*. A year later she picked up a second award for *Kill Bill: Volume 2*.

actresses with the most mtv movie awards

awards won

4	4	4	3	3
Alicia Silverstone	Kristen Stewart	Uma Thurman	Drew Barrymore	Kirsten Dunst

Kristen Stewart

Stan Lee

Appearing in 15 movies since he debuted as an actor in 1995, Stan Lee rules the box office with an average gross of $192.6 million per movie. Some of his biggest films include the Spider-Man trilogy, which earned a combined $2.5 billion worldwide. Lee is the co-creator of the Spider-Man comic book series for Marvel Comics, and was given small parts in all of the films. He also helped create the Iron Man, Fantastic Four, X-Men, and Hulk comic books, and was able to appear in those films as well. Lee has been honored for his work numerous times, including induction into the Jack Kirby Hall of Fame. His latest film, *Iron Man 2*, earned $623 million in 2010.

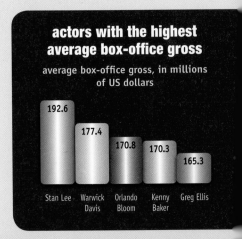

actors with the highest average box-office gross

average box-office gross, in millions of US dollars

Stan Lee	Warwick Davis	Orlando Bloom	Kenny Baker	Greg Ellis
192.6	177.4	170.8	170.3	165.3

actor with the highest career box-office gross

Frank Welker

Frank Welker's movies have a combined total gross of $5.72 billion. Although movie fans might not recognize Welker's name or face, they would probably recognize one of his voices. Welker is a voice actor, and has worked on more than 90 movies in the last 25 years. Some of his most famous voices include Megatron, Curious George, and Scooby-Doo. Welker's most profitable movies include *How the Grinch Stole Christmas*, *Godzilla*, and *101 Dalmatians*.

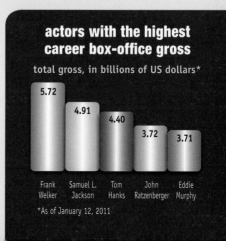

actors with the highest career box-office gross

total gross, in billions of US dollars*

Frank Welker	Samuel L. Jackson	Tom Hanks	John Ratzenberger	Eddie Murphy
5.72	4.91	4.40	3.72	3.71

*As of January 12, 2011

movies

top-grossing animated movie

Toy Story 3

With earnings of more than $1.06 billion worldwide, *Toy Story 3* has easily become the highest-grossing animated movie in history. It is also the fifth-highest-grossing movie ever. The Disney-Pixar movie opened on June 18, 2010, and earned $110 million during its first three days in theaters. The plot of the third installment of the Toy Story franchise follows Woody as he leads the other toys out of a daycare center where they were mistakenly delivered. The toys' famous voices included Tom Hanks (Woody), Tim Allen (Buzz), Joan Cusack (Jessie), and John Ratzenberger (Hamm).

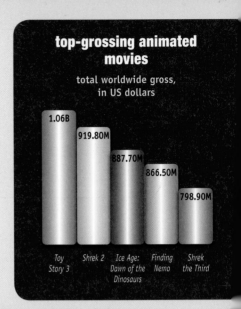

top-grossing animated movies

total worldwide gross, in US dollars

Toy Story 3	Shrek 2	Ice Age: Dawn of the Dinosaurs	Finding Nemo	Shrek the Third
1.06B	919.80M	887.70M	866.50M	798.90M

movie with the most successful opening weekend

Harry Potter and the Deathly Hallows: Part 2

When *Harry Potter and the Deathly Hallows: Part 2* debuted on July 15, 2011, the eighth installment of the wizard phenomenon hauled in $169.1 million over three days. The movie also claimed the record for the biggest opening day of all time, with a gross of $92 million. The final film in the Harry Potter series starred Daniel Radcliffe as Harry, Emma Watson as Hermione, and Rupert Grint as Ron. Together they search for Lord Voldemort's Horcruxes in an effort to finally defeat him. Combined, the Harry Potter movies have earned more than $7 billion worldwide.

movies with the most successful opening weekends
weekend earnings, in millions of US dollars

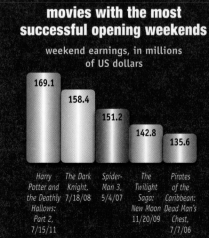

169.1	158.4	151.2	142.8	135.6
Harry Potter and the Deathly Hallows: Part 2, 7/15/11	The Dark Knight, 7/18/08	Spider-Man 3, 5/4/07	The Twilight Saga: New Moon 11/20/09	Pirates of the Caribbean: Dead Man's Chest, 7/7/06

movies

top-grossing movie

Avatar

Avatar, James Cameron's science-fiction epic, was released in December 2009 and grossed more than $2.78 billion worldwide in less than two months. Starring Sigourney Weaver, Sam Worthington, and Zoe Saldana, *Avatar* cost more than $230 million to make. Cameron began working on the film in 1994, and it was eventually filmed in 3-D, with special cameras made just for the movie. Due to *Avatar*'s overwhelming success, Cameron is already planning two sequels.

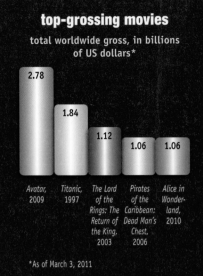

top-grossing movies

total worldwide gross, in billions of US dollars*

2.78	1.84	1.12	1.06	1.06
Avatar, 2009	Titanic, 1997	The Lord of the Rings: The Return of the King, 2003	Pirates of the Caribbean: Dead Man's Chest, 2006	Alice in Wonder-land, 2010

*As of March 3, 2011

most successful movie franchise

Harry Potter

The first seven movies in the Harry Potter franchise have collectively earned $6.35 billion. The series, which began in November 2001, is based on the bestselling books by J. K. Rowling. They chronicle the adventures of a young wizard—Harry Potter—as he grows up and learns of the great power he possesses. The highest-grossing movie in the franchise is the first one—*Harry Potter and the Sorcerer's Stone*—which earned $974 million worldwide. The leads of the movie, including Daniel Radcliffe, Rupert Grint, and Emma Watson, have become some of the highest-paid young stars in Hollywood.

most successful movie franchises

total worldwide gross,
in billions of US dollars

Harry Potter	Star Wars	James Bond	Shrek	The Lord of the Rings
6.35	5.49	3.55	2.94	2.91

*As of March 3, 2011

movies

top-earning actor

Johnny Depp

Johnny Depp banked $75 million for his work in two successful movies in 2010. Depp starred as the Mad Hatter in Tim Burton's *Alice in Wonderland*, which earned more than $1 billion at the box office. In December 2010, Depp starred with Angelina Jolie in *The Tourist*. He was nominated for a Golden Globe for Best Actor in a Comedy or Musical for both films. Depp also earned nominations for an MTV Movie Award, a National Movie Award, and a Teen Choice Award for *Alice in Wonderland*. Depp has had an equally strong 2011. His animated film *Rango* released in March 2011 and *Pirates of Caribbean: On Stranger Tides* released in May.

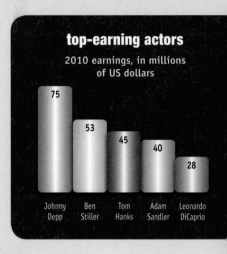

top-earning actors

2010 earnings, in millions
of US dollars

Johnny Depp	Ben Stiller	Tom Hanks	Adam Sandler	Leonardo DiCaprio
75	53	45	40	28

top-earning actress
Sandra Bullock

Between June 2009 and June 2010, Sandra Bullock earned $56 million. *The Proposal* hit theaters in June 2009 and made more than $317 million worldwide. A few months later, *The Blind Side* debuted and grossed $309 million worldwide. For her work on the movie, Bullock was awarded a Golden Globe, a SAG Award, and an Academy Award. With more than 30 movies to her credit, Bullock has a box-office receipt total of $3.2 billion worldwide. Bullock is also well-known for her charity work. She has donated millions of dollars to the American Red Cross and other relief organizations.

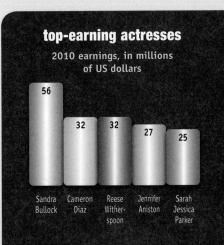

top-earning actresses
2010 earnings, in millions of US dollars

Sandra Bullock	Cameron Diaz	Reese Witherspoon	Jennifer Aniston	Sarah Jessica Parker
56	32	32	27	25

highest animated movie budget

Tangled

Walt Disney Animated Studios budgeted $260 million for its latest fairy-tale remake, *Tangled*—and the big bucks paid off. *Tangled* nearly doubled that figure with a worldwide gross of $480 million. Animators used computer-generated imagery (CGI) to create the film, but it was also combined with hand-drawn images to resemble classic fairy-tale films. Released in 2010, *Tangled* follows the journey of Rapunzel, from her tower deep in the forest to a reunion with her long-lost family. Mandy Moore, Zachary Levi, and Donna Murphy lent their voices to the main characters.

highest animated movie budgets

budget, in millions of US dollars

260	200	200	180	175
Tangled, 2010	Disney's A Christmas Carol, 2009	Toy Story 3, 2010	WALL-E, 2008	Up, 2009

highest movie budget

Pirates of the Caribbean: At World's End

With a budget of $300 million, the creators of *Pirates of the Caribbean: At World's End* spent the most money in movie history. And all of that money seems to have paid off. The third installment of the Pirates series opened in May 2007 and has since earned more than $960 million worldwide. It is the fifth-highest-grossing movie worldwide, and had the fourth-highest domestic gross in 2007. The Jerry Bruckheimer blockbuster starred Johnny Depp as Captain Jack Sparrow, Orlando Bloom as Will Turner, and Keira Knightley as Elizabeth Swann.

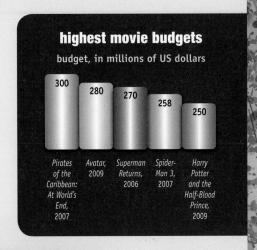

highest movie budgets

budget, in millions of US dollars

300	280	270	258	250
Pirates of the Caribbean: At World's End, 2007	Avatar, 2009	Superman Returns, 2006	Spider-Man 3, 2007	Harry Potter and the Half-Blood Prince, 2009

movies

The Twilight Saga: New Moon

Summit Entertainment's second installment of the Twilight Saga—*New Moon*—earned a record $72.7 million on November 20, 2009. The movie also earned the most money during a midnight screening with $26.3 million. The vampire romance movie was released in 4,024 theaters, with an average gross of $18,068 per theater. Many theaters were already sold out of tickets for the premiere two months before the big day. The movie went on to earn more than $295 million in the United States and a total of $705.5 million worldwide. *New Moon* starred Robert Pattinson, Kristen Stewart, and Taylor Lautner.

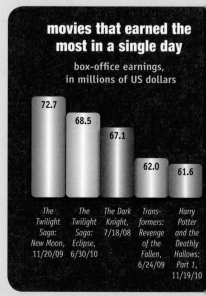

movies that earned the most in a single day

box-office earnings, in millions of US dollars

72.7	68.5	67.1	62.0	61.6
The Twilight Saga: New Moon, 11/20/09	The Twilight Saga: Eclipse, 6/30/10	The Dark Knight, 7/18/08	Trans-formers: Revenge of the Fallen, 6/24/09	Harry Potter and the Deathly Hallows: Part 1, 11/19/10

top-selling dvd

Avatar

With more than 10.1 million copies sold, *Avatar* was by far the bestselling DVD of 2010. DVD sales totaled $183.2 million since its release date in April 2010, and *Avatar* was among the top-ten bestselling DVDs for the 14 weeks. The science-fiction film directed by James Cameron hit theaters in December 2009. The cast included Sam Worthington, Stephen Lang, Sigourney Weaver, Michelle Rodriguez, Zoë Saldana, and Giovanni Ribisi. With the film's huge success, Cameron announced that he would release sequels to Avatar in 2014 and 2015.

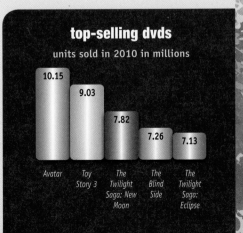

top-selling dvds

units sold in 2010 in millions

10.15	9.03	7.82	7.26	7.13
Avatar	Toy Story 3	The Twilight Saga: New Moon	The Blind Side	The Twilight Saga: Eclipse

movies

James Cameron

James Cameron, who is one of the most successful directors in movie-making history, earned $210 million in 2010. Most of Cameron's earnings came from his 2009 blockbuster *Avatar*—the top-grossing film of all time and the top-selling DVD of 2010. Since his directorial debut in 1978, Cameron's movies have earned a worldwide box office total of $5.6 billion. Some of his most successful films include *Titanic* ($1.84 billion), *True Lies* ($365 million), and *Terminator 2: Judgment Day* ($516 million). In 1997, Cameron won three Academy Awards for his work on *Titanic*.

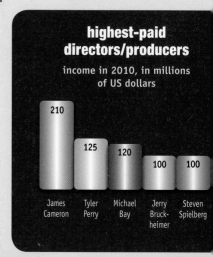

highest-paid directors/producers

income in 2010, in millions of US dollars

James Cameron	Tyler Perry	Michael Bay	Jerry Bruck-heimer	Steven Spielberg
210	125	120	100	100

bestselling movie soundtrack

The Bodyguard

The soundtrack of *The Bodyguard* has sold more than 17 million copies since it was released in November 1992. The movie starred Kevin Costner as a former FBI agent in charge of a pop singer, played by Whitney Houston. Houston produced the soundtrack, along with Clive Davis, and it features three of Houston's biggest hits—"I Will Always Love You," "I Have Nothing," and "I'm Every Woman." The album picked up a Grammy for Album of the Year and reached number one on music charts worldwide, including Australia, Canada, France, Germany, and Japan.

bestselling movie soundtracks

units sold, in millions

The Bodyguard	Saturday Night Fever	Purple Rain	Forrest Gump	Titanic
17	15	13	12	11

music

bestselling album

Recovery

Eminem had enormous success with his latest album, *Recovery*. It sold more than 3.4 million copies in 2010. The album, which was released in June, debuted at number one on the Billboard 200 chart and remained there for seven weeks. The three top singles from *Recovery* include, "No Love," "Not Afraid," and "Love the Way You Lie." The album received ten Grammy nominations in 2010, including Album of the Year and Best Rap Album. *Rolling Stone* also ranked *Recovery* ninth in its list of 2010's Best Albums of the Year.

bestselling albums

units sold in 2010

3,415,000	3,089,000	2,960,000	2,319,000	1,852,000
Recovery, Eminem	*Need You Now*, Lady Antebellum	*Speak Now*, Taylor Swift	*My World 2.0*, Justin Bieber	*The Gift*, Susan Boyle

most downloaded recording artist

Eminem

Fans downloaded more than 15.6 million copies of Eminem's songs in 2010. The rapper kicked off 2010 with the release of his seventh album, *Recovery*. The first single off the album, "Not Afraid," entered the Billboard Hot 100 at number one, and sold more than 3.4 million downloads in 2010. The album's second single, "Love the Way You Lie," features Rihanna, and was released in May. It debuted at number two on the Billboard Hot 100, and sold more than 4.25 million downloads in 2010.

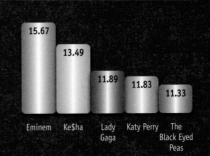

most downloaded recording artists

songs downloaded in 2010, in millions

Eminem	Ke$ha	Lady Gaga	Katy Perry	The Black Eyed Peas
15.67	13.49	11.89	11.83	11.33

most downloaded song

"California Gurls"

Katy Perry's "California Gurls" sold 4.39 million copies online in 2010. Fans downloaded the summer anthem more than 2 million times in the first seven weeks of release, making it the second-fastest-selling digital song in history (behind Flo Rida's "Right Round"). The single was the first release on Perry's second album, *Teenage Dream*, and features rapper Snoop Dogg. "California Gurls" hit number one on the Billboard Hot 100, and remained there for six straight weeks. The song became Perry's second US number-one single, after "I Kissed a Girl" in 2008. "California Gurls" also became a number-one hit in many other countries, including Canada, Australia, Hungary, and Ireland.

most downloaded songs

downloads in 2010, in millions

"California Gurls," Katy Perry	"Hey, Soul Sister," Train	"Love the Way You Lie," Eminem	"Dyna-mite," Taio Cruz	"Air-planes," B.o.B.
4.39	4.31	4.24	4.08	4.00

top-selling recording artist

Taylor Swift

Taylor Swift sold a total of 4.47 million copies of her albums in 2010. This includes Swift's latest album, *Speak Now*, which sold 2.96 million copies and was the third bestselling album of the year. The album's first single, "Mine," entered the Billboard Hot 100 at number three. Swift's first two albums—*Taylor Swift* and *Fearless*—were also extremely successful, and Swift was named top-selling recording artist in 2008 as well. Since her career began, Swift has won four Grammy Awards and has sold more than 16 million records worldwide. In 2009, at the age of 19, she became the youngest winner of the CMA's Entertainer of the Year Award.

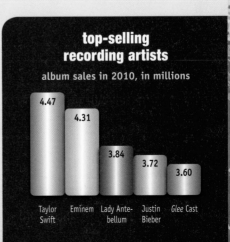

top-selling recording artists

album sales in 2010, in millions

Taylor Swift	Eminem	Lady Antebellum	Justin Bieber	*Glee* Cast
4.47	4.31	3.84	3.72	3.60

united states' bestselling recording group

The Beatles

The Beatles have sold 177 million copies of their albums in the United States since their first official recording session in September 1962. In the two years that followed, they had 26 Top 40 singles. John Lennon, Paul McCartney, George Harrison, and Ringo Starr made up the "Fab Four," as the Beatles were known. Together they recorded many albums that are now considered rock masterpieces, such as *Rubber Soul*, *Sgt. Pepper's Lonely Hearts Club Band*, and *The Beatles*. The group broke up in 1969. In 2001, however, their newly released greatest hits album—*The Beatles 1*—reached the top of the charts. One of their best-known songs—"Yesterday"—is the most recorded song in history, with about 2,500 different artists recording their own versions.

united states' bestselling recording groups

albums sold, in millions

The Beatles	Led Zeppelin	The Eagles	Pink Floyd	AC/DC
177.0	111.5	100.0	74.5	71.0

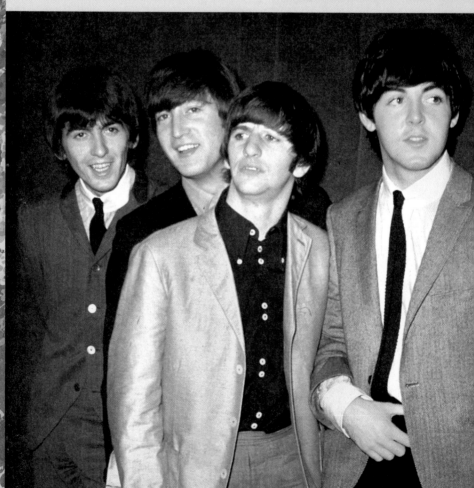

top-earning hip-hop artist

Jay-Z

Rapper Jay-Z earned $63 million in 2010. Some of his millions are from his eleventh studio album, *The Blueprint 3*, which was released in late 2009. He also joined Eminem in June for two sold-out concerts in New York and Detroit called The Home & Home Tour. Jay-Z published his own memoir, *Decoded*, in November. In addition to his book and music, Jay-Z is also a successful entrepreneur. He is part owner of the New Jersey Nets basketball team and owns a chain of sports restaurants located in airports across the country.

top-earning hip-hop artists

earnings in 2010, in millions of US dollars

Artist	Earnings
Jay-Z	63
Sean (Diddy) Combs	30
Akon	21
Lil Wayne	20
Dr. Dre	17

music

bestselling digital song of all time

"I Gotta Feeling"

The Black Eyed Peas' mega dance hit "I Gotta Feeling" is the bestselling digital song of all time with more than 6.6 million downloads. The song, which was released in May 2009, is from The Black Eyed Peas' fifth studio album, *The E.N.D.* "I Gotta Feeling" won a Grammy Award for Best Pop Performance by a Duo or Group, and was nominated for Song of the Year at the World Music Awards. The song was number one on the Billboard Hot 100 chart for 12 straight weeks and also topped music charts in 25 other countries. The members of the group are will.i.am, apl.de.ap, Taboo, and Stacy "Fergie" Ferguson.

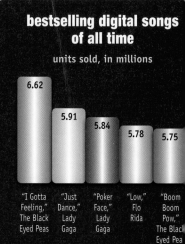

bestselling digital songs of all time

units sold, in millions

6.62	5.91	5.84	5.78	5.75
"I Gotta Feeling," The Black Eyed Peas	"Just Dance," Lady Gaga	"Poker Face," Lady Gaga	"Low," Flo Rida	"Boom Boom Pow," The Black Eyed Pea

bestselling digital album of all time

21

21—the second studio album from Adele—has become the most downloaded album of all time, with 1 million copies sold. The record has also sold more than 8 million hard copies worldwide, with about half of those sales in the United States. 21's lead single, "Rolling in the Deep," has sold more than 4.23 million digital copies worldwide. The single was first released in November 2010 and has reached number one on the charts in six countries, including the United States. Adele, a singer and songwriter from England, is known for her unique blend of folk, R&B, country, and blues styles.

bestselling digital albums of all time

total digital albums sold

1M	884,000	852,000	795,000	700,000
21, Adele	The Fame, Lady Gaga	Recovery, Eminem	Viva La Vida, Coldplay	Fearless, Taylor Swift

top-earning male singer
Bruce Springsteen

Bruce Springsteen earned $70 million in 2010. Springsteen, also known as "the Boss," hit the road with his E Street Band and sold more than 2 million concert tickets for his world tour. With a gross of more than $167 million, it became the third-highest-grossing tour in the world during 2010. Later in the year, a documentary about one of Springsteen's early albums—*Darkness on the Edge of Town*—was created for the Toronto International Film Festival, and it also aired on HBO. His 17th studio album, *The Promise*, featured new songs based on that earlier album.

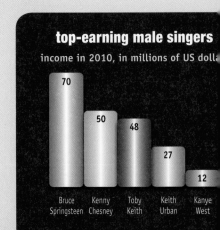

top-earning male singers
income in 2010, in millions of US dolla

Bruce Springsteen	Kenny Chesney	Toby Keith	Keith Urban	Kanye West
70	50	48	27	12

top-earning female singer

Beyoncé

In 2010, Beyoncé was the 87-million-dollar woman, thanks in part to her I Am . . . Tour. The tour, which wrapped up early that year, earned $103 million. Beyoncé also led in Grammy Award nominations in 2010, with ten. She won six. In addition to her music, Beyoncé has multiple business deals. In 2005, Beyoncé cofounded House of Deréon—a ready-to-wear fashion line. She also launched her own fragrance in 2010 called Heat. Beyoncé also has several highly profitable endorsement deals, including L'Oréal and Nintendo.

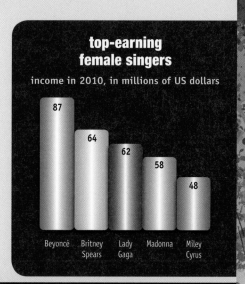

top-earning female singers

income in 2010, in millions of US dollars

Beyoncé	Britney Spears	Lady Gaga	Madonna	Miley Cyrus
87	64	62	58	48

music

most played song

"Need You Now"

"Need You Now," the first single released off Lady Antebellum's album with the same title, was the most-played song of 2010 with 600,000 radio detections, or times a song was played on air. The song, which won Song of the Year and Single of the Year at the Academy of Country Music Awards, spent five weeks at number one on the Billboard Hot Country Songs chart. It also became a hit in the pop world, and reached number two on the Billboard Hot 100 chart. "Need You Now" was certified quadruple platinum by the Recording Industry Association of America. In 2010, "Need You Now" won Song of the Year at the Grammy Awards.

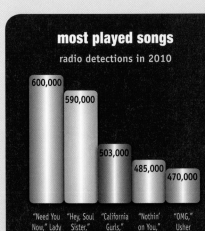

most played songs

radio detections in 2010

600,000	590,000	503,000	485,000	470,000
"Need You Now," Lady Antebellum	"Hey, Soul Sister," Train	"California Gurls," Katy Perry	"Nothin' on You," B.o.B.	"OMG," Usher

bestselling ringtone
"Need You Now"

Country music sensation Lady Antebellum released their second studio album—*Need You Now*—and its lead single became the best-selling ringtone of that year, according to the Billboard/Nielsen data. The album sold about 481,000 copies in the first week of release, and it has been certified as triple platinum by the Recording Industry Association of America. The album debuted at number one on the Billboard 200 chart, and featured several other popular tracks, including "Our Kind of Love," "American Honey," and "Hello World." *Need You Now* also received a Grammy nomination for Album of the Year.

bestselling ringtones

billboard rating

1	2	3	4	5
"Need You Now," Lady Antebellum	"Bedrock," Young Money	"Love the Way You Lie," Eminem featuring Rihanna	"Tik Tok," Ke$ha	"Smile," Uncle Kracker

top-earning tour

Bon Jovi

After kicking off in February 2010, Bon Jovi's The Circle tour earned $146.5 million. The band, which includes singer Jon Bon Jovi, guitarist Richie Sambora, keyboardist David Bryan, drummer Tico Torres, and bassist Hugh McDonald, took home about $51.9 million of the proceeds. During The Circle tour, the band played 69 venues, and the first 35 US dates were sold out. The band also had some other notable moments along the way, becoming the first band to play at the new Meadowlands Stadium in their home state of New Jersey, and the first to play on the roof of the O2 Arena in London.

top-earning tours

earnings in 2010, in millions of US dollars

Bon Jovi	U2	AC/DC	Lady Gaga	The Black Eyed Peas
146.5	131.5	122.6	116.2	81.5

act with the most country music awards

George Strait

George Strait has won a whopping 22 Country Music Awards and has been nicknamed the "King of Country" for all of his accomplishments in the business. He won his first CMA award in 1985, and his most recent in 2008. In addition to his many awards, Strait holds the record for the most number one hits on the Billboard Hot Country Songs with 44. He also has 38 hit albums, including 12 multiplatinum and 22 platinum records. He was inducted into the Country Music Hall of Fame in 2006.

acts with the most country music awards

awards won

George Strait	Brooks & Dunn	Vince Gill	Alan Jackson	Brad Paisley
22	19	18	16	14

musician with the most mtv video music awards

Madonna

Madonna has won 20 MTV Video Music Awards since the ceremony was first held in 1984. She has won four Cinematography awards, three Female Video awards, three Directing awards, two Editing awards, and two Art Direction awards. She also picked up single awards for Video of the Year, Choreography, Special Effects, and Long Form Video, as well as a Viewer's Choice and a Video Vanguard Award. Madonna's award-winning videos include "Papa Don't Preach," "Like a Prayer," "Express Yourself," "Vogue," "Rain," "Take a Bow," "Ray of Light," and "Beautiful Stranger."

musicians with the most mtv video music awards

awards won

Madonna	Peter Gabriel	R.E.M.	Eminem	Lady Gaga
20	13	12	12	11

play with the most tony awards

The Producers

In March 2001, *The Producers* took home 12 of its record-breaking 15 Tony Award nominations. The Broadway smash won awards for Musical, Original Score, Book, Direction of a Musical, Choreography, Orchestration, Scenic Design, Costume Design, Lighting Design, Actor in a Musical, Featured Actor in a Musical, and Actress in a Musical. *The Producers*, which originally starred Nathan Lane and Matthew Broderick, is a stage adaptation of Mel Brooks's 1968 movie. Brooks wrote the lyrics and music for 16 new songs for the stage version.

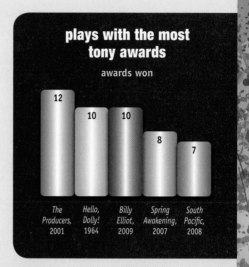

plays with the most tony awards
awards won

The Producers, 2001	Hello, Dolly! 1964	Billy Elliot, 2009	Spring Awakening, 2007	South Pacific, 2008
12	10	10	8	7

theater

longest-running broadway show

The Phantom of the Opera

The Phantom of the Opera has been performed more than 9,567 times since it opened in January 1988. The show tells the story of a disfigured musical genius who terrorizes the performers of the Paris Opera House. More than 100 million people have seen a performance in 144 cities and 27 countries. The show won seven Tony Awards its opening year, including Best Musical. The musical drama is performed at the Majestic Theater.

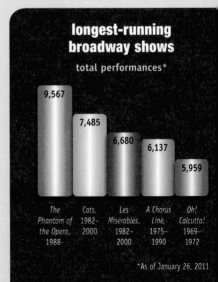

longest-running broadway shows

total performances*

	9,567	7,485	6,680	6,137	5,959
	The Phantom of the Opera, 1988–	Cats, 1982–2000	Les Misérables, 1982–2000	A Chorus Line, 1975–1990	Oh! Calcutta! 1969–1972

*As of January 26, 2011

sports records

basketball • football • bicycling • golf
baseball • track & field • tennis • olympics
soccer • car racing • motorcycling • horse racing
hockey • x games • snowboarding

nba team with the most championship titles

Boston Celtics

The Boston Celtics are the most successful team in the NBA with 17 championship wins. The first win came in 1957, and the team went on to win the next seven consecutive titles—the longest streak of consecutive championship wins in the history of US sports. The most recent championship title came in 2008. The Celtics entered the Basketball Association of America in 1946, which later merged into the NBA in 1949. The Celtics made the NBA play-offs for four consecutive seasons from 2001 to 2005, but they were eliminated in early rounds each time.

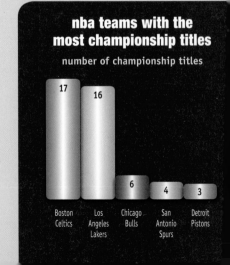

nba teams with the most championship titles

number of championship titles

Boston Celtics	Los Angeles Lakers	Chicago Bulls	San Antonio Spurs	Detroit Pistons
17	16	6	4	3

Wilt Chamberlain & Michael Jordan

Both Michael Jordan and Wilt Chamberlain averaged an amazing 30.1 points per game during their legendary careers. Jordan played for the Chicago Bulls and the Washington Wizards. He led the league in scoring for seven years. During the 1986 season, he became the second person ever to score 3,000 points in a single season. Chamberlain played for the Philadelphia Warriors, the Philadelphia 76ers, and the Los Angeles Lakers. In addition to the highest scoring average, he holds the record for the most games with 50 or more points, with 118.

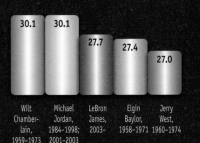

nba players with the highest career scoring averages

average points per game

30.1	30.1	27.7	27.4	27.0
Wilt Chamberlain, 1959–1973	Michael Jordan, 1984–1998; 2001–2003	LeBron James, 2003–	Elgin Baylor, 1958–1971	Jerry West, 1960–1974

Michael Jordan

nba's highest-scoring game

Detroit Pistons

On December 13, 1983, the Detroit Pistons beat the Denver Nuggets with a score of 186–184 at McNichols Arena in Denver, Colorado. The game was tied at 145 at the end of regular play, and three overtime periods were needed to determine the winner. During the game, both the Pistons and the Nuggets each had six players who scored in the double figures. Four players scored more than 40 points each, which was an NBA first. The Pistons scored 74 field goals that night, claiming another NBA record that still stands today.

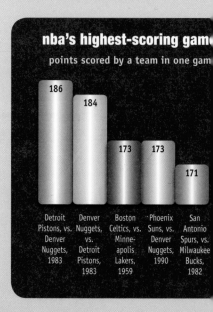

nba's highest-scoring game

points scored by a team in one game

186	184	173	173	171
Detroit Pistons, vs. Denver Nuggets, 1983	Denver Nuggets, vs. Detroit Pistons, 1983	Boston Celtics, vs. Minneapolis Lakers, 1959	Phoenix Suns, vs. Denver Nuggets, 1990	San Antonio Spurs, vs. Milwaukee Bucks, 1982

nba player with the highest salary

Kobe Bryant

Kobe Bryant earns $24.8 million a year playing as a guard for the LA Lakers. Bryant has been a Laker since he turned pro in 1996. During his 14 years in the NBA, he has scored more than 27,700 points and grabbed more than 5,800 rebounds. Bryant has also logged almost 40,000 minutes on the court. He is a five-time NBA Champion between 2000 and 2010, and he was the NBA Most Valuable Player during the 2007–2008 season. He has also earned All-NBA honors every year since 2002. In 2008, Bryant helped Team USA win the gold medal at the Beijing Olympics.

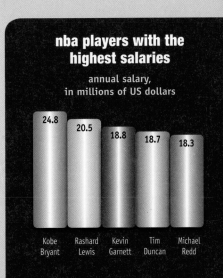

nba players with the highest salaries

annual salary,
in millions of US dollars

Kobe Bryant	Rashard Lewis	Kevin Garnett	Tim Duncan	Michael Redd
24.8	20.5	18.8	18.7	18.3

nba player with the most career points

Kareem Abdul-Jabbar

During his highly successful career, Kareem Abdul-Jabbar scored a total of 38,387 points. In 1969, Abdul-Jabbar began his NBA tenure with the Milwaukee Bucks. He was named Rookie of the Year in 1970. The following year he scored 2,596 points and helped the Bucks win the NBA championship. He was traded to the Los Angeles Lakers in 1975, and with his new team, Abdul-Jabbar won the NBA championship in 1980, 1982, 1985, 1987, and 1988. He retired from basketball in 1989 and was inducted into the Basketball Hall of Fame in 1995.

nba players with the most career points

points scored

Kareem Abdul-Jabbar, 1969–1989	Karl Malone, 1985–2004	Michael Jordan, 1984–1998; 2001–2003	Wilt Chamberlain, 1959–1973	Shaquille O'Neal, 1992–
38,387	36,928	32,292	31,419	28,590

wnba player with the highest career ppg average

Cynthia Cooper

Cynthia Cooper has the highest scoring average in the WNBA with 21 points per game. During the play-offs, she has averaged 23.3 points per game. Cooper joined the league in 1997 as a Houston Comet and remained there for four years. After a two-year hiatus, she returned for a year, and then retired in 2003. During her five years in the WNBA, she scored a total of 2,601 points. Cooper has a career high of 44 points in one game versus Sacramento in 1997. She won a gold medal in the 1988 Olympics in Seoul, the 1987 Pan American Games, and the 1990 FIBA World Championship.

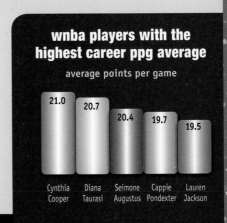

wnba players with the highest career ppg average

average points per game

Cynthia Cooper	Diana Taurasi	Seimone Augustus	Cappie Pondexter	Lauren Jackson
21.0	20.7	20.4	19.7	19.5

wnba player with the most career points

Tina Thompson

A nine-time WNBA All-Star, Tina Thompson has scored 6,413 points during her 14-year career. The Los Angeles Sparks forward began her WNBA career in 1997 with the Houston Comets. She was the first draft pick in WNBA history. During her first four years with the Comets, she helped the team win the WNBA Championship each season and was the 2000 All-Star MVP. She joined the Los Angeles Sparks in 2009, and has a points per game average of 16.1. At the 2004 and 2008 Olympic Games, Thompson picked up gold medals for her role in helping Team USA dominate the competition.

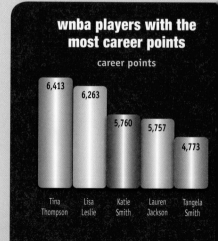

wnba players with the most career points

career points

Tina Thompson	Lisa Leslie	Katie Smith	Lauren Jackson	Tangela Smith
6,413	6,263	5,760	5,757	4,773

UConn Women

The University of Connecticut's Huskies won 90 consecutive games between April 2008 and December 2010. After losing to Stanford in the 2008 NCAA semifinals, the UConn women's team started their next season with a win and continued their victory streak right through the national championship. The Huskies then started the 2009–2010 season ranked number one, and won every game up to their streak-ending loss to Stanford on December 19, 2010. During this streak, the team won by an average of 25 points per game. The UConn women have won a total of six NCAA championships.

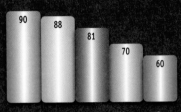

longest ncaa basketball streaks

consecutive games won

90	88	81	70	60
UConn women, 2008–2010	UCLA men, 1971–1974	Washington–St. Louis women, 1998–2001	UConn women, 2001–2003	San Francisco men, 1955–1957

basketball

women's basketball team with the most ncaa championships

Tennessee

The Tennessee Lady Volunteers have won eight NCAA basketball championships. The Lady Vols won their latest championship in 2008. In 1998, they had a perfect record of 39–0, which was the most seasonal wins ever in women's collegiate basketball at the time. In 2004, Tennessee was in the championship but was beaten by the University of Connecticut Huskies. Since 1976, an impressive 14 Lady Vols have been to the Olympics, and 5 Lady Vols have been inducted into the Women's Basketball Hall of Fame in Knoxville, Tennessee.

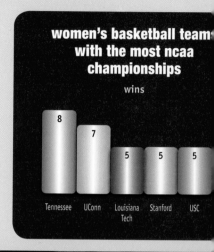

women's basketball team with the most ncaa championships

wins

Tennessee	UConn	Louisiana Tech	Stanford	USC
8	7	5	5	5

men's basketball team with the most ncaa championships

UCLA

With 11 titles, the University of California, Los Angeles (UCLA) has the most NCAA basketball championship wins. The Bruins won their 11th championship in 1995. The school has won 23 of their last 41 league titles and has been in the NCAA play-offs for 35 of the last 41 years. During the final round of the NCAA championship in 2006, UCLA lost to the Florida Gators with a score of 73–57. Not surprisingly, UCLA has produced some basketball legends, including Kareem Abdul-Jabbar, Reggie Miller, and Baron Davis. For the last 36 years, the Bruins have called Pauley Pavilion home.

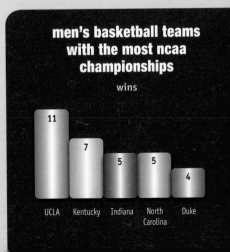

men's basketball teams with the most ncaa championships

wins

UCLA	Kentucky	Indiana	North Carolina	Duke
11	7	5	5	4

nfl player with the most passing yards

Brett Favre

Quarterback Brett Favre knows how to hit his receivers: He completed 71,838 passing yards during his amazing career. He has a completion rate of 62 percent, and has connected for 508 touchdowns. Favre is also the NFL's all-time leader in passing touchdowns (508), completions (6,300), and attempts (10,169). Favre began his career with the Atlanta Falcons in 1991. He was traded to the Green Bay Packers the next season, and played for them until 2007. Favre joined the New York Jets for the season, and was then signed by the Minnesota Vikings for the 2009 season.

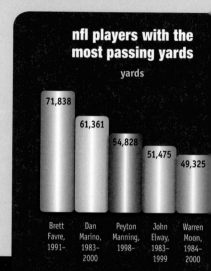

nfl players with the most passing yards
yards

Brett Favre, 1991–	Dan Marino, 1983–2000	Peyton Manning, 1998–	John Elway, 1983–1999	Warren Moon, 1984–2000
71,838	61,361	54,828	51,475	49,325

nfl player with the highest career rushing total

Emmitt Smith

Running back Emmitt Smith holds the record for all-time rushing yards with 18,355. Smith began his career with the Dallas Cowboys in 1990 and played with the team until the end of the 2002 season. In 2003, Smith signed a two-year contract with the Arizona Cardinals. Smith also holds the NFL records for the most carries with 4,142 and the most rushing touchdowns with 164. After 15 years in the NFL, Smith retired at the end of the 2004 season.

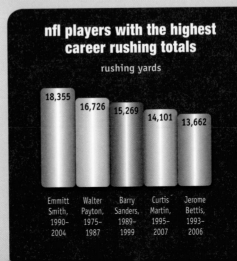

nfl players with the highest career rushing totals

rushing yards

Emmitt Smith, 1990–2004	Walter Payton, 1975–1987	Barry Sanders, 1989–1999	Curtis Martin, 1995–2007	Jerome Bettis, 1993–2006
18,355	16,726	15,269	14,101	13,662

Jerry Rice

Jerry Rice has scored a record 208 touchdowns. He is widely considered to be one of the greatest wide receivers to ever play in the National Football League. Rice holds a total of 14 NFL records, including career receptions (1,549), receiving yards (22,895), receiving touchdowns (197), consecutive 100-catch seasons (4), most games with 100 receiving yards (73), and many others. He was named NFL Player of the Year twice, *Sports Illustrated* Player of the Year four times, and NFL Offensive Player of the Year once. Rice retired from the NFL in 2005.

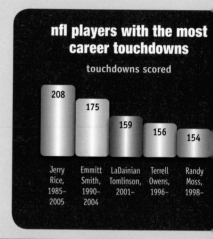

nfl players with the most career touchdowns

touchdowns scored

Jerry Rice, 1985–2005	Emmitt Smith, 1990–2004	LaDainian Tomlinson, 2001–	Terrell Owens, 1996–	Randy Moss, 1998–
208	175	159	156	154

nfl player with the most single-season touchdowns

LaDainian Tomlinson

Running back LaDainian Tomlinson scored 31 touchdowns during the 2006 season. He was also named NFL Most Valuable Player that season for his outstanding performance. During his pro career, he has scored a total of 138 touchdowns. Tomlinson was selected fifth overall in the 2001 draft by the San Diego Chargers but was traded to the New York Jets in 2010. He holds several Chargers records, including 372 attempts (2002), 100 receptions (2003), and 1,815 rushing yards in a season (2006). Tomlinson has also been named to five Pro Bowls.

nfl players with the most single-season touchdowns

touchdowns scored

LaDainian Tomlinson, 2006	Shaun Alexander, 2005	Priest Holmes, 2003	Marshall Faulk, 2000	Emmitt Smith, 1995
31	28	27	26	25

nfl player with the highest career scoring total

Morten Andersen

Morten Andersen led the NFL in scoring with a career total of 2,544 points. He made 565 field goals out of 709 attempts, giving him a 79.9 percent completion rate. He scored 849 extra points out of 859 attempts, resulting in a 98.8 percent success rate. Andersen, a placekicker who began his career in 1982 with the New Orleans Saints, retired in 2008 after playing for the Atlanta Falcons. Known as the Great Dane, partly because of his birthplace of Denmark, Andersen played 382 professional games. His most successful season was in 1995, when he scored 122 points.

nfl players with the highest career scoring totals

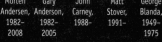

points scored

Morten Andersen, 1982–2008	Gary Anderson, 1982–2005	John Carney, 1988–	Matt Stover, 1991–	George Blanda, 1949–1975
2,544	2,434	2,062	2,004	2,002

nfl team with the most super bowl wins

Pittsburgh Steelers

With six championship wins between 1974 and 2009, the Pittsburgh Steelers have won more Super Bowls than any other team in NFL history. The Steelers have also played and won more AFC championship games than any other team in the conference. The Steelers were founded in 1933 and are the fifth-oldest franchise in the league. Twenty-three retired Steelers have been inducted into the Pro Football Hall of Fame, including Franco Harris, Chuck Noll, and Terry Bradshaw.

nfl teams with the most super bowl wins

super bowls won

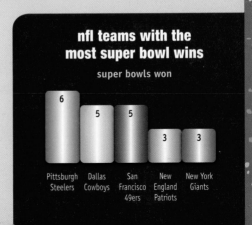

Pittsburgh Steelers	Dallas Cowboys	San Francisco 49ers	New England Patriots	New York Giants
6	5	5	3	3

football

Don Shula

Don Shula led his teams to a remarkable 347 wins during his 33 years as a head coach in the National Football League. When Shula became head coach of the Baltimore Colts in 1963, he became the youngest head coach in football history. He stayed with the team until 1969 and reached the play-offs four times. Shula became the head coach for the Miami Dolphins in 1970 and coached them until 1995. During this time, the Dolphins reached the play-offs 20 times and won at least 10 games a season 21 times. After leading them to Super Bowl wins in 1972 and 1973, Shula became one of only five coaches to win the championship in back-to-back years.

nfl coaches with the most wins

games won

347	324	270	229	209
Don Shula, 1963–1995	George Halas, 1922–1929; 1933–1941; 1946–1955; 1958–1967	Tom Landry, 1960–1988	Curly Lambeau, 1919–1957	Chuck Noll, 1969–1991

nfl player with the highest salary

Peyton Manning

Peyton Manning's salary of $23 million tops all other players' in the NFL. The Indianapolis Colts quarterback has played with the team since he joined the league in 1998. He has a career average rating of 94.9 and achieved his highest rating of 121.1 in 2004. Manning holds the team records for career passing yards, career wins, pass completions, and passing touchdowns. He also holds the NFL record for the most MVP Awards, with four, which he received between 2003 and 2009. Manning has been selected to the Pro Bowl 11 times, and won the Super Bowl in 2006 against the Chicago Bears.

nfl players with the highest salaries

annual salary, in millions of US dollars

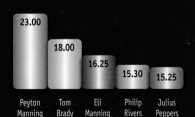

Peyton Manning	Tom Brady	Eli Manning	Philip Rivers	Julius Peppers
23.00	18.00	16.25	15.30	15.25

nfl team with the most consecutive wins

New England Patriots

Between 2006 and 2007, the New England Patriots won 19 consecutive games. They ended the 2006 regular season with three wins. During the 2007 regular season, the team won all 16 games—only the fifth team in league history to do so. During this impressive season, the team set an NFL record by scoring 589 points and 75 touchdowns. The Patriots have a winning history, including 10 AFC East championships, 15 NFL play-off appearances, and 3 Super Bowl wins.

nfl teams with the most consecutive wins
consecutive games won

19	18	17	17	16
New England Patriots, 2006–2007	New England Patriots, 2003–2004	Chicago Bears, 1933–1934	Miami Dolphins, 1972–1973	Chicago Bears, 1941–1942

cyclist with the most tour de france wins

Lance Armstrong

Lance Armstrong was the first cyclist ever to win seven Tour de France races. He won his first race in 1999, just three years after being diagnosed with cancer. He went on to win the top cycling event for the next six years, retiring after his 2005 victory. Armstrong has received many awards and honors during his career, including being named *Sports Illustrated*'s Sportsman of the Year in 2002. Armstrong also formed the Lance Armstrong Foundation, which supports people recovering from cancer.

cyclists with the most tour de france wins
number of wins

Lance Armstrong, USA	Eddy Merckx, Belgium	Jacques Anquetil, France	Bernard Hinault, France	Miguel Indurain, Spain
7	5	5	5	5

pga golfer with the lowest seasonal average

Matt Kuchar

American golfer Matt Kuchar had the lowest seasonal scoring average in 2010 with 69.43. He has played in 240 events since he joined the PGA Tour in 2000. Of those events, Kuchar won three of them, and landed in the top 10 for 37 events. He also had a first-place finish on the Nationwide Tour in 2006. He was part of the US Ryder Cup Team in 2010 and has won $14.4 million during his career. Before turning pro, Kuchar won the 1997 US Amateur Championship while attending Georgia Tech. In 1998, he won the Fred Haskins Award, which is given to the country's best collegiate golfer.

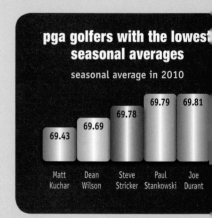

pga golfers with the lowest seasonal averages

seasonal average in 2010

Matt Kuchar	Dean Wilson	Steve Stricker	Paul Stankowski	Joe Durant
69.43	69.69	69.78	69.79	69.81

Ipga golfer with the lowest seasonal average

Na Yeon Choi

South Korean golfer Na Yeon Choi won the Vare Trophy for achieving the lowest seasonal scoring average in 2010 with 69.87. In 2010, Choi led the tour in birdies (338), percentage of rounds under par (72.2 percent), and sand saves (67.3 percent). She was also the Official Money List leader with $1.87 million in winnings that year. Choi joined the LPGA in 2008, and has earned nearly $5 million in career winnings since then. She has played in 81 LPGA events and posted 4 wins and 36 top-ten finishes. Choi also played on the Korean LPGA Tour and won six championships there.

Ipga golfers with the lowest seasonal averages

seasonal average in 2010

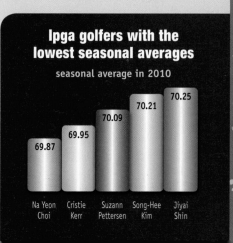

Na Yeon Choi	Cristie Kerr	Suzann Pettersen	Song-Hee Kim	Jiyai Shin
69.87	69.95	70.09	70.21	70.25

lpga's highest-paid golfer

Annika Sorenstam

Annika Sorenstam has earned $22.5 million since her LPGA career began in 1994. During this time, she has had 72 career victories, including 9 majors. In 2005, Sorenstam earned her eighth Rolex Player of the Year award—the most in LPGA history. She also became the first player to sweep Rolex Player of the Year honors, the Vare Trophy, and the ADT Official Money List title five times. Sorenstam earned her fifth consecutive Mizuno Classic title, making her the first golfer in LPGA history to win the same event five consecutive years. Sorenstam retired at the end of the 2008 season.

lpga's highest-paid golfers

career earnings, in millions of US dollars

Annika Sorenstam	Karrie Webb	Lorena Ochoa	Cristie Kerr	Juli Inkster
22.5	16.2	14.8	12.1	11.7

Jack Nicklaus

Golfing great Jack Nicklaus has won a total of 18 major championships. His wins include six Masters, five PGAs, four US Opens, and three British Opens. Nicklaus was named PGA Player of the Year five times. He was a member of the winning US Ryder Cup team six times and was an individual World Cup winner a record three times. He was inducted into the World Golf Hall of Fame in 1974, just 12 years after he turned professional. He joined the US Senior PGA Tour in 1990. In addition to playing the game, Nicklaus has designed close to 200 golf courses and has written a number of popular books about the sport.

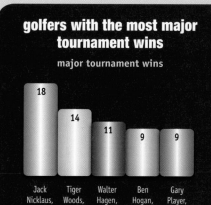

golfers with the most major tournament wins

major tournament wins

Jack Nicklaus, 1962–1986	Tiger Woods, 1997–	Walter Hagen, 1914–1929	Ben Hogan, 1946–1953	Gary Player, 1959–1978
18	14	11	9	9

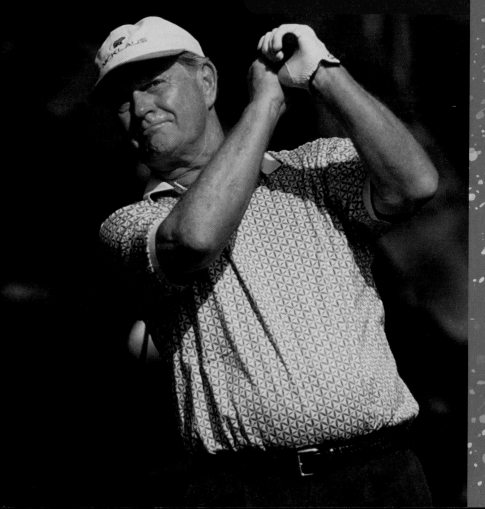

baseball

mlb player with the highest seasonal home-run total

Barry Bonds

On October 5, 2001, Barry Bonds smashed Mark McGwire's record for seasonal home runs when he hit his 71st home run in the first inning of a game against the Los Angeles Dodgers. In the third inning, he hit number 72, and two days later he reached 73. Bonds, a left fielder for the San Francisco Giants, has a career total of 762 home runs. He also holds the records for seasonal walks (232) and seasonal on-base percentage (.609). Bonds and his father, hitting coach Bobby Bonds, hold the all-time father-son home-run record with 1,020.

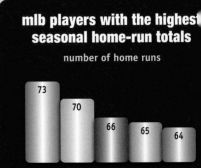

mlb players with the highest seasonal home-run totals

number of home runs

Barry Bonds, 2001	Mark McGwire, 1998	Sammy Sosa, 1998	Mark McGwire, 1999	Sammy Sosa, 2001
73	70	66	65	64

mlb player with the most home runs

Barry Bonds

Barry Bonds has hit more home runs than anyone who ever played in the MLB, cracking 762 balls over the wall during his ongoing career. Bonds has hit more than 30 home runs in a season 13 times—another MLB record. During his impressive career, Bonds has won 8 Gold Gloves, 12 Silver Slugger awards, and 13 All-Star awards. Bonds began his career with the Pittsburgh Pirates in 1986; he was transferred to the San Francisco Giants in 1993 and has played for the team since then. He is only one of three players to join the 700 Home Run Club.

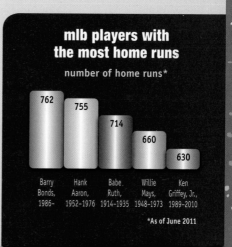

mlb players with the most home runs

number of home runs*

Barry Bonds, 1986–	Hank Aaron, 1952–1976	Babe Ruth, 1914–1935	Willie Mays, 1948–1973	Ken Griffey, Jr., 1989–2010
762	755	714	660	630

*As of June 2011

Nolan Ryan

Nolan Ryan leads Major League Baseball with an incredible 5,714 career strikeouts. In his impressive 28-year career, he played for the New York Mets, the California Angels, the Houston Astros, and the Texas Rangers. The right-handed pitcher from Refugio, Texas, led the American League in strikeouts ten times. In 1989, at the age of 42, Ryan became the oldest pitcher ever to lead the Major Leagues in strikeouts. Ryan set another record in 1991 when he pitched his seventh career no-hitter.

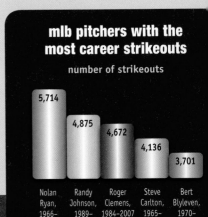

mlb pitchers with the most career strikeouts
number of strikeouts

Nolan Ryan, 1966–1993	Randy Johnson, 1989–2009	Roger Clemens, 1984–2007	Steve Carlton, 1965–1988	Bert Blyleven, 1970–1992
5,714	4,875	4,672	4,136	3,701

mlb player with the most career hits

Pete Rose

Pete Rose belted an amazing 4,256 hits during his 23 years of professional baseball. He made his record-setting hit in 1985, when he was a player-manager for the Cincinnati Reds. By the time Rose retired as a player from Major League Baseball in 1986, he had set several other career records. Rose holds the Major League records for the most career games (3,562), the most times at bat (14,053), and the most seasons with more than 200 hits (10). During his career, he played for the Cincinnati Reds, the Philadelphia Phillies, and the Montreal Expos.

**mlb players with
the most career hits**

number of hits

4,256	4,191	3,771	3,630	3,514
Pete Rose, 1963–1986	Ty Cobb, 1905–1928	Hank Aaron, 1952–1976	Stan Musial, 1941–1963	Tris Speaker, 1907–1928

mlb team with the highest payroll

New York Yankees

The combined 2011 payroll of the New York Yankees totals more than $206 million. Some of the highest-paid players include Alex Rodriguez ($32 million), C. C. Sabathia ($24.2 million), and Mark Teixeira ($23.1 million). The Yankees have been very successful with their pricey roster, winning 40 American League pennants and 27 World Series. The team also has a new place to showcase its talent—a new Yankee Stadium opened in 2009. The stadium cost $1.5 billion, making it the second-most expensive stadium in the world.

mlb teams with the highest payrolls

payroll in 2011, in millions of US dolla

New York Yankees	Boston Red Sox	Chicago Cubs	Philadelphia Phillies	New York Mets
206.7	160.9	146.6	142.7	136.0

Rickey Henderson

During his 25 years in the majors, baseball great Rickey Henderson boasts the most career runs with 2,295. Henderson got his start with the Oakland Athletics in 1979, and went on to play for the Yankees, the Mets, the Mariners, the Red Sox, the Padres, the Dodgers, and the Angels. Henderson won a Gold Glove award in 1981, and the American League MVP award in 1989 and 1990. Henderson is also known as the "Man of Steal" because he holds the MLB record for most stolen bases in a career, with 1,406.

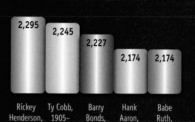

mlb players with the most career runs

number of career runs

Rickey Henderson, 1979–2003	Ty Cobb, 1905–1928	Barry Bonds, 1986–	Hank Aaron, 1954–1976	Babe Ruth, 1914–1935
2,295	2,245	2,227	2,174	2,174

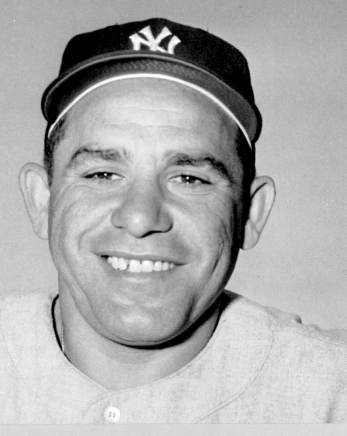

Yogi Berra

most mvp awards in the american league

Yogi Berra, Joe DiMaggio, Jimmie Foxx, Mickey Mantle, & Alex Rodriguez

With three honors each, Yogi Berra, Joe DiMaggio, Jimmie Foxx, Mickey Mantle, and Alex Rodriguez all hold the record for the Most Valuable Player awards during their professional careers. Berra, DiMaggio, Mantle, and Rodriguez were all New York Yankees. Foxx played for the Athletics, the Cubs, and the Phillies. The player with the biggest gap between wins was DiMaggio, who won his first award in 1939 and his last in 1947. Also nicknamed "Joltin' Joe" and the "Yankee Clipper," DiMaggio began playing in the Major Leagues in 1936. The following year, he led the league in home runs and runs scored. He was inducted into the Baseball Hall of Fame in 1955.

mlb players with the most american league mvp awards

number of mvp awards

Yogi Berra, 1946–1963; 1965	Joe DiMaggio, 1936–1951	Jimmie Foxx, 1925–1945	Mickey Mantle, 1951–1968	Alex Rodriguez, 1994–
3	3	3	3	3

Barry Bonds

San Francisco Giant Barry Bonds has earned seven Most Valuable Player awards for his amazing achievements in the National League. He received his first two MVP awards in 1990 and 1992 while playing for the Pittsburgh Pirates. The next five awards came while wearing the Giants uniform in 1993, 2001, 2002, 2003, and 2004. Bonds is the first player to win an MVP award three times in consecutive seasons. In fact, Bonds is the only baseball player in history to have won more than three MVP awards.

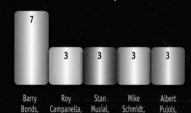

mlb players with the most national league mvp awards

number of mvp awards

Barry Bonds, 1986–	Roy Campanella, 1948–1957	Stan Musial, 1941–1963	Mike Schmidt, 1972–1989	Albert Pujols, 2001–
7	3	3	3	3

baseball

New York Yankees

Between 1923 and 2010, the New York Yankees were the World Series champions a record 27 times. The team picked up their latest win in October of 2009 when they beat the Philadelphia Phillies. The Yankees beat the Phillies four games to two to get their first win in nine years. Since their early days, the team has included some of baseball's greatest players, including Babe Ruth, Lou Gehrig, Yogi Berra, Joe DiMaggio, and Mickey Mantle.

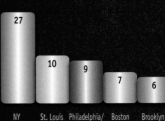

mlb teams with the most world series wins

number of wins

NY Yankees	St. Louis Cardinals	Philadelphia/ Kansas City/ Oakland Athletics	Boston Red Sox	Brooklyn/ LA Dodgers
27	10	9	7	6

mlb pitcher with the most cy young awards

Roger Clemens

Roger Clemens, a starting pitcher for the
Houston Astros, has earned a record seven
Cy Young Awards during his career so far.
He set a Major League record in April 1986
when he struck out 20 batters in one game.
He later tied this record in September 1996.
In September 2001, Clemens became the first
Major League pitcher to win 20 of his first
21 decisions in one season. In June 2003,
he became the first pitcher in more than a
decade to win his 300th game. He also struck
out his 4,000th batter that year.

mlb pitchers with the most cy young awards

number of cy young awards

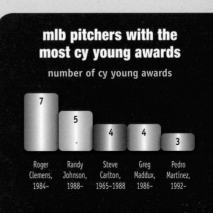

Roger Clemens, 1984–	Randy Johnson, 1988–	Steve Carlton, 1965–1988	Greg Maddux, 1986–	Pedro Martinez, 1992–
7	5	4	4	3

mlb player with the most at bats

Pete Rose

Pete Rose has stood behind the plate for 14,053 at bats—more than any other Major League player. Rose signed with the Cincinnati Reds after graduating from high school in 1963, and played second base. During his impressive career, Rose set several other records, including the most singles in the Major Leagues (3,315), most seasons with 600 or more at bats in the Major Leagues (17), most career doubles in the National League (746), and most career runs in the National League (2,165). He was also named World Series MVP, *Sports Illustrated*'s Sportsman of the Year, and the *Sporting News* Man of the Year.

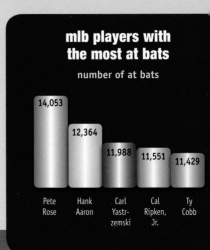

mlb players with the most at bats

number of at bats

Pete Rose	Hank Aaron	Carl Yastr-zemski	Cal Ripken, Jr.	Ty Cobb
14,053	12,364	11,988	11,551	11,429

mlb player with the most career RBIs

Hank Aaron

During his 23 years in the Major Leagues, right-handed Hank Aaron batted in an incredible 2,297 runs. Aaron began his professional career with the Indianapolis Clowns, a team in the Negro American League, in 1952. He was traded to the Milwaukee Braves in 1954 and won the National League batting championship with an average of .328. He was named the league's Most Valuable Player a year later when he led his team to a World Series victory. Aaron retired as a player in 1976 and was inducted into the Baseball Hall of Fame in 1982.

mlb players with the most career RBIs

number of runs batted in

Hank Aaron, 1952–1976	Babe Ruth, 1914–1935	Cap Anson, 1876–1897	Barry Bonds, 1986–	Lou Gehrig, 1923–1939
2,297	2,213	2,076	1,996	1,995

mlb player with the most consecutive games played

Cal Ripken, Jr.

Baltimore Oriole Cal Ripken, Jr., played 2,632 consecutive games from May 30, 1982, to September 20, 1998. The right-handed third baseman also holds the record for the most consecutive innings played: 8,243. In June 1996, Ripken broke the world record for consecutive games with 2,216, surpassing Sachio Kinugasa of Japan. When he played as a shortstop, Ripken set Major League records for most home runs (345) and most extra base hits (855) for his position. He started in the All-Star Game a record 19 times in a row.

mlb players with the most consecutive games played

number of consecutive games played

Cal Ripken, Jr., 1978–2001	Lou Gehrig, 1923–1939	Everett Scott, 1914–1925	Steve Garvey, 1968–1988	Miguel Tejada, 1997–
2,632	2,130	1,307	1,207	1,152

runner with the fastest mile

Hicham El Guerrouj

Moroccan runner Hicham El Guerrouj is super-speedy—he ran a mile in just over 3 minutes and 43 seconds in July 1999 while racing in Rome. He also holds the record for the fastest mile in North America with a time just short of 3 minutes and 50 seconds. El Guerrouj is an Olympian with gold medals in the 1,500-meter and 5,000-meter races. With this accomplishment at the 2004 Athens games, he became the first runner to win both races at the same Olympics in more than 75 years. El Guerrouj returned to the Olympics in 2006 as a torchbearer in Torino, Italy.

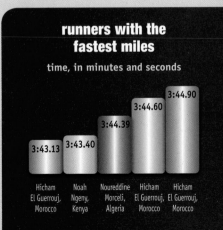

runners with the fastest miles

time, in minutes and seconds

3:43.13	3:43.40	3:44.39	3:44.60	3:44.90
Hicham El Guerrouj, Morocco	Noah Ngeny, Kenya	Noureddine Morceli, Algeria	Hicham El Guerrouj, Morocco	Hicham El Guerrouj, Morocco

top-earning female tennis player

Serena Williams

Serena Williams has earned $32.7 million since she began playing professional tennis in 1995. During her amazing career, Williams has won 37 singles championships and 20 doubles championships, as well as two gold medals in the 2000 and 2008 Olympics. She has also won all four of the Grand Slam championships. Williams has won many impressive awards, including AP's Female Athlete of the Year, the BBC's Sports Personality of the Year, and two Espy Awards.

top-earning female tennis players

career earnings, in millions of US dollars

32.7	27.7	23.6	22.1	21.8
Serena Williams, 1995–	Venus Williams, 1994–	Kim Clijsters 1997–	Lindsay Davenport, 1993–	Steffi Graf, 1982–1999

top-earning male tennis player

Roger Federer

Tennis great Roger Federer has earned $62 million since his career began in 1998. He has won 67 singles titles and 8 doubles titles, including 16 Grand Slams. His major victories include four Australian Opens, one French Open, six Wimbledon titles, and five US Opens. From February 2, 2004, to August 17, 2008, Federer was ranked first in the world for 237 consecutive weeks. He is also the only player in history to win five consecutive titles at two different Grand Slam tournaments (Wimbledon and US Open).

top-earning male tennis players

career earnings, in millions of US dollars

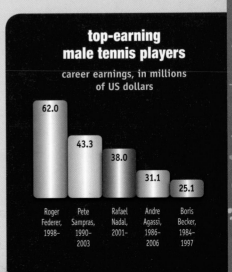

Roger Federer, 1998–	Pete Sampras, 1990–2003	Rafael Nadal, 2001–	Andre Agassi, 1986–2006	Boris Becker, 1984–1997
62.0	43.3	38.0	31.1	25.1

woman with the most grand slam singles titles

Margaret Court Smith

Margaret Court Smith won 24 Grand Slam singles titles between 1960 and 1975. She is the only woman ever to win the French, British, US, and Australian titles during one year in both the singles and doubles competitions. She was only the second woman to win all four singles titles in the same year. During her amazing career, she won a total of 66 Grand Slam championships—more than any other woman. Court was the world's top-seeded female player from 1962 to 1965, 1969 to 1970, and 1973. She was inducted into the International Tennis Hall of Fame in 1979.

women with the most grand slam singles titles

number of titles won

24	22	19	18	18
Margaret Court Smith, 1960–1975	Steffi Graf, 1987–1999	Helen Wills-Moody, 1923–1938	Chris Evert, 1974–1986	Martina Navratilova, 1975–1995

Roger Federer

Swiss tennis great Roger Federer has won a record 16 Grand Slam championship titles and earned more than $55.4 million since he turned pro in 1998. He has four Australian Open wins, one French Open win, six Wimbledon wins, and five US Open wins. Federer is also one of only two players to win the Golden Slam—winning all four Grand Slam championships and an Olympic gold medal in the same year (2008). Federer ended 2009 as the ATP World Tour Champion for the fifth time in six years.

men with the most grand slam singles titles

number of titles won

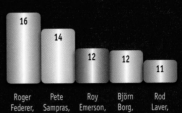

Roger Federer, 2003–	Pete Sampras, 1990–2002	Roy Emerson, 1961–1967	Björn Borg, 1974–1981	Rod Laver, 1960–1969
16	14	12	12	11

man with the fastest olympic 200-meter freestyle

Michael Phelps

Swimmer superstar Michael Phelps completed the 200-meter freestyle in just under 1 minute and 43 seconds during the 2008 Beijing Olympics. At that Olympics, he also won a record eight gold medals. When they are added to the six gold and two bronze medals he won at the Athens games in 2004, his medal count totals 16—the second highest in Olympic history. Phelps was named World Swimmer of the Year six times, and American Swimmer of the Year eight times. In 2008, Phelps was also named *Sports Illustrated* magazine's Sportsman of the Year.

men with the fastest olympic 200-meter freestyle

total time, in minutes and seconds

1:42.96	1:44.71	1:45.35	1:46.70	1:47.25
Michael Phelps, USA	Ian Thorpe, Australia	Pieter van den Hoogenband, Netherlands	Yevgeny Sadovyi, Unified Team	Duncan Armstrong, Australia

woman with the fastest olympic
200-meter freestyle

Federica Pellegrini

Italian swimmer Federica Pellegrini swam
the 200-meter freestyle at Beijing in 2008
in Olympic record time (1:54.82). Just a
year later, she broke the world record for
the 200-meter freestyle (1:52.98) as well.
Pelligrini is not only a one-event wonder. An
accomplished 400-meter freestyle swimmer
as well, she became the first woman to
complete that event in less than 4 minutes.
The first Italian woman to become an
Olympic champion, Pellegrini is also the first
Italian swimmer to hold records in more than
one event. At the 2004 Athens Olympics, she
became the youngest Italian athlete to win
a medal when she took the silver in the 200-
meter freestyle at the age of 16.

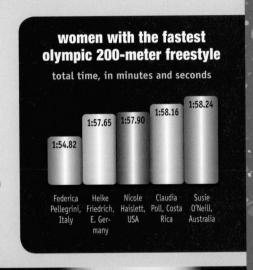

women with the fastest olympic 200-meter freestyle

total time, in minutes and seconds

Federica Pellegrini, Italy	Heike Friedrich, E. Germany	Nicole Haislett, USA	Claudia Poll, Costa Rica	Susie O'Neill, Australia
1:54.82	1:57.65	1:57.90	1:58.16	1:58.24

man with the fastest olympic 100-meter dash

Usain Bolt

Jamaican sprinter Usain Bolt ran the 100-meter dash in less than 10 seconds during the 2008 Beijing Olympics. In 2009, he ran 100 meters in just 8.7 seconds during a 150-meter race. He holds the Olympic and world records in the 200-meter race and the 4x100 relay. Nicknamed "Lightning Bolt," he has been awarded IAAF World Athlete of the Year, Track & Field Athlete of the Year, and Laureus Sportsman of the Year. In addition to his three gold Olympic medals from Beijing, Bolt also has three gold medals from the 2009 track and field world championship.

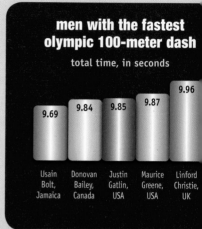

men with the fastest olympic 100-meter dash

total time, in seconds

9.69	9.84	9.85	9.87	9.96
Usain Bolt, Jamaica	Donovan Bailey, Canada	Justin Gatlin, USA	Maurice Greene, USA	Linford Christie, UK

woman with the fastest olympic 100-meter dash

Florence Griffith Joyner

Florence Griffith Joyner—also known as "Flo Jo"—broke the 100-meter Olympic record at the 1988 Seoul Olympics with a time of 10.54 seconds, and was a gold medalist in the 4x100 meter relay as well. The world record holder for both the 100-meter (10.49) and 200-meter (21.34), she is considered by many to be the fastest woman of all time. In addition to her gold medals from Seoul, Griffith Joyner has two silver medals—one from the 1988 Olympics in the 4x400 meter relay, and one from the 1984 Los Angeles Games for the 200-meter dash. In 1998, Florence Griffith Joyner died following an epileptic seizure. She was 38 years old.

women with the fastest olympic 100-meter dash

total time, in seconds

Florence Griffith Joyner, USA	Shelly-Ann Fraser, Jamaica	Gail Devers, USA	Yuliya Nesterenko, Belarus	Gail Devers, USA
10.54	10.78	10.82	10.93	10.94

country with the most gymnastics gold medals in women's all-around competition

Russia

Russian athletes have dominated the female all-around competition in gymnastics, winning seven gold medals between 1956 and 1992. The champions—who competed under Russian and Soviet Union flags—include Tatiana Gutsu (1992), Elena Shushunova (1988), Elena Davydova (1980), Lyudmila Turishcheva (1972), and Larisa Latynina (1956, 1960). Latynina is the only female athlete in the world to win nine gold medals and is the most medaled Olympic athlete in the world with 18. The women's all-around competition began at the 1952 games in Helsinki.

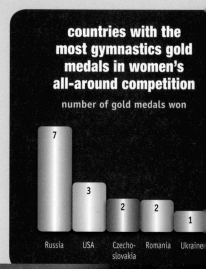

countries with the most gymnastics gold medals in women's all-around competition

number of gold medals won

Russia	USA	Czecho-slovakia	Romania	Ukraine
7	3	2	2	1

Tatiana Gutsu

soccer player with the highest salary

Lionel Messi

Lionel Messi earns a whopping $39.6 million a year for playing striker/winger for La Liga's Barcelona team. Messi has won the Ballon d'Or and been named the FIFA World Player of the Year. During the 2004 season, the 17-year-old Messi made history by becoming the youngest person to score a goal in La Liga. Two years later, he became the youngest Argentinean to play in the FIFA World Cup. In 2008, Messi competed at the Olympics in Beijing and brought home the gold medal with the Argentinean team. He has scored 13 goals in international competition.

soccer players with the highest salaries

annual salary, in millions of US dollars

Lionel Messi, Barcelona	David Beckham, LA Galaxy	Cristiano Ronaldo, Real Madrid	Kaka, Real Madrid	Thierry Henry, Barcelona
39.6	36.5	36.0	22.6	21.7

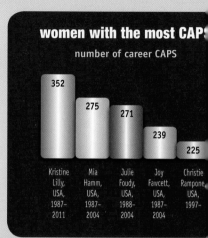

woman with the most CAPS
Kristine Lilly

With a total of 352, Kristine Lilly holds the world record for the most international games played, or CAPS. This is the highest number of CAPS in both the men's and women's international soccer organizations. She has a career total of 130 international goals—the second highest in the world. In 2004, Lilly scored her 100th international goal, becoming one of only five women to ever accomplish that feat. In 2005, Lilly was named US Soccer's Female Athlete of the Year. She retired in January 2011.

women with the most CAPS
number of career CAPS

352	275	271	239	225
Kristine Lilly, USA, 1987–2011	Mia Hamm, USA, 1987–2004	Julie Foudy, USA, 1988–2004	Joy Fawcett, USA, 1987–2004	Christie Rampone, USA, 1997–

man with the most CAPS

Mohamed Al-Deayea

Saudi Arabian soccer great Mohamed Al-Deayea has the most international games, or CAPs. Al-Deayea began his professional career as a goalie with the Saudi team Al-Ta'ee in 1991 and played there for nine years. In 2000, he became the captain of Al-Hilal. While playing as a part of the Saudi national team, Al-Deayea reached the World Cup three times between 1994 and 2002. He was placed on the 2006 World Cup team but did not play in any games. At the end of the competition, Al-Deayea announced his retirement.

men with the most CAPS

number of career CAPS

181	178	175	169	164
Mohamed Al-Deayea, Saudi Arabia, 1990–2006	Claudio Suárez, Mexico, 1992–2010	Ahmed Hassan, Egypt, 1995–	Hossam Hassan, Egypt, 1985–2007	Cobi Jones, USA, 1992–2007

country with the most world cup points

Germany

Germany has accumulated a total of 33 points during World Cup soccer competition. A win is worth 4 points, runner-up is worth 3 points, third place is worth 2 points, and fourth place is worth 1 point. Germany won the World Cup four times between 1954 and 1990. Most recently, Germany earned 2 points for a third-place finish in 2010. The World Cup is organized by the Fédération Internationale de Football Association (FIFA) and is played every four years.

countries with the most world cup points

total number of points

Germany/ W. Germany, 1954– 2006	Brazil, 1958– 2002	Italy, 1934– 2006	Argentina, 1978– 1986	Uruguay, 1930– 1950
33	30	25	14	10

driver with the most formula one wins

Michael Schumacher

Race-car driver Michael Schumacher won 91 Formula One races in his professional career, which began in 1991. Out of the 250 races he competed in, he reached the podium 154 times. In 2002, Schumacher became the only Formula One driver to have a podium finish in each race in which he competed that season. He won seven world championships between 1994 and 2004. Schumacher, who was born in Germany, began his career with Benetton but later switched to Ferrari. He retired from racing in 2006.

drivers with the most formula one wins

number of wins

Michael Schumacher	Alain Prost	Ayrton Senna	Nigel Mansell	Jackie Stewart
91	51	41	31	27

driver with the fastest daytona 500 win

Buddy Baker

Race-car legend Buddy Baker dominated the competition at the 1980 Daytona 500 with an average speed of over 177 miles (285 km) per hour. It was the first Daytona 500 race run under three hours. Baker had a history of speed before this race—he became the first driver to race more than 200 miles (322 km) per hour on a closed course in 1970. During his amazing career, Baker competed in 688 Winston Cup races—he won 19 of them and finished in the top five in 198 others. He also won more than $3.6 million. He was inducted into the International Motorsports Hall of Fame in 1997.

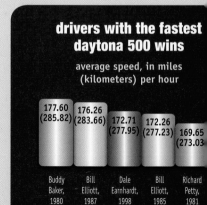

drivers with the fastest daytona 500 wins

average speed, in miles (kilometers) per hour

Buddy Baker, 1980	Bill Elliott, 1987	Dale Earnhardt, 1998	Bill Elliott, 1985	Richard Petty, 1981
177.60 (285.82)	176.26 (283.66)	172.71 (277.95)	172.26 (277.23)	169.65 (273.03

Jimmie Johnson

Jimmie Johnson has won five consecutive
Sprint Cup Championships between 2006 and
2010. With his 54 series wins, he is ranked 10th
in career victories. During his career, Johnson
has also had 138 top-five finishes and 208
top-ten finishes. He has been named Driver of
the Year four times, which is a record he holds
with teammate Jeff Gordon. Johnson joined the
Hendrick Motorsports team in 2002, and drives
a Chevrolet owned by Gordon. In addition to
his Sprint Cup victories, Johnson has won the
Daytona 500 one time and the Coca-Cola 500
and the All State 400 three times each.

**drivers with the most
consecutive sprint cup
championships**

consecutive wins

Jimmie Johnson, 2006–2010	Cale Yarborough, 1976–1978	Jeff Gordon, 1997–1998	Dale Earnhardt 1993–1994	Darrell Waltrip 1981–1982
5	3	2	2	2

Jimmie
Johnson

WINNER
June 28, 2009

youngest driver to win a sprint cup race

Joey Logano

A little over a month after his 19th birthday, Joey Logano became the youngest winner of a Sprint Cup race. He accomplished this on June 28, 2009, in New Hampshire. Later that year, he also became the youngest recipient of the Raybestos Rookie of the Year Award. In 2010, Logano became the youngest pole winner in Sprint Cup history at Bristol Motor Speedway. He drives a Toyota for the Joe Gibbs Racing Team, which is sponsored by The Home Depot. Logano began his NASCAR career in 2007, and won seven races on six different tracks that year.

youngest drivers to win a sprint cup race
age at time of win

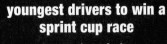

19 years, 35 days	20 years, 1 day	20 years, 125 days	20 years, 129 days	21 years, 205 days
Joey Logano, 2009	Trevor Bayne, 2011	Kyle Busch, 2005	Donald Thomas, 1952	Fireball Roberts, 1950

Stefan Everts

Stefan Everts is the king of motocross with a total of ten world titles. He won twice on a 500cc bike, seven more times on a 250cc bike, and once on a 125cc bike. During his 18-year career, he had 101 Grand Prix victories. Everts was named Belgium Sportsman of the Year five times. He retired after his final world title in 2006 and is now a consultant and coach for the riders who compete for the KTM racing team.

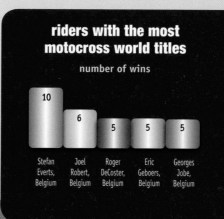

riders with the most motocross world titles

number of wins

Stefan Everts, Belgium	Joel Robert, Belgium	Roger DeCoster, Belgium	Eric Geboers, Belgium	Georges Jobe, Belgium
10	6	5	5	5

motorcycling

rider with the most superbike race points

Max Biaggi

Italian superbike racer Max Biaggi earned 451 points during the 2010 racing season. Biaggi began racing 125cc class motorcycles in 1989, eventually moving up to superbike racing in 2007. He was on the Alstare Corona Suzuki team and won his first race at the Losail International Circuit. In 2009, he began racing with his current team—Aprilia. In 2010, he became both the first Italian racer and the first racer from Aprilia to win the World Superbike Championship. During his career, Biaggi has competed in 214 professional races and won 42 of them.

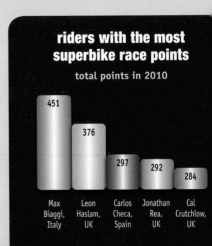

riders with the most superbike race points

total points in 2010

Max Biaggi, Italy	Leon Haslam, UK	Carlos Checa, Spain	Jonathan Rea, UK	Cal Crutchlow, UK
451	376	297	292	284

Eddie Arcaro

Between 1938 and 1961, jockey Eddie Arcaro won a total of 17 Triple Crown races. Nicknamed "the Master," Arcaro won the Kentucky Derby five times, the Preakness six times, and the Belmont six times. He holds the record for the most Preakness wins, and is tied for the most Kentucky Derby and Belmont wins. He was also horse racing's top money winner six times between 1940 and 1955. During his career, Arcaro competed in 24,092 races and won 4,779 of them.

jockeys with the most triple crown wins

number of wins

Eddie Arcaro	Bill Shoemaker	Bill Hartack	Earl Sande	Pat Day
17	11	9	9	9

hockey

Montreal Canadiens

The Montreal Canadiens won an amazing 24 Stanley Cup victories between 1916 and 1993. That's almost one-quarter of all the Stanley Cup championships ever played. The team plays at Montreal's Molson Centre. The Canadiens were created in December 1909 by J. Ambrose O'Brien to play for the National Hockey Association (NHA). They eventually made the transition into the National Hockey League. Over the years, the Canadiens have included such great players as Maurice Richard, George Hainsworth, Jacques Lemaire, Saku Koivu, and Emile Bouchard.

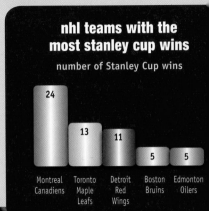

nhl teams with the most stanley cup wins

number of Stanley Cup wins

Montreal Canadiens	Toronto Maple Leafs	Detroit Red Wings	Boston Bruins	Edmonton Oilers
24	13	11	5	5

nhl player with the most career points

Wayne Gretzky

Wayne Gretzky scored an unbelievable 2,857 points and 894 goals during his 20-year career. Gretzky was the first person in the NHL to average more than two points per game. Many people consider Canadian-born Gretzky to be the greatest player in the history of the National Hockey League. In fact, he is called "the Great One." He officially retired from the sport in 1999 and was inducted into the Hockey Hall of Fame that same year. After his final game, the NHL retired his jersey number (99). In 2005, Gretzky became the head coach of the Phoenix Coyotes.

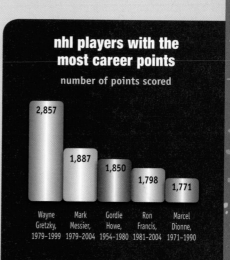

nhl players with the most career points

number of points scored

2,857	1,887	1,850	1,798	1,771
Wayne Gretzky, 1979–1999	Mark Messier, 1979–2004	Gordie Howe, 1954–1980	Ron Francis, 1981–2004	Marcel Dionne, 1971–1990

nhl goalie with the most career wins

Martin Brodeur

Not much gets by goalie Martin Brodeur—he's won 624 games since he was drafted by the New Jersey Devils in 1990. Still playing with the Devils, Brodeur has helped the team win three Stanley Cup championships. He is also the only goalie in NHL history to complete seven seasons with 40 or more wins. Brodeur has been an NHL All-Star ten times, and has received the Vezina Trophy and the Jennings Trophy four times each. He also ranks second in the league in regular-season shutouts.

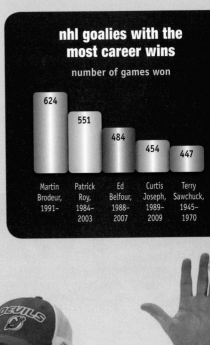

nhl goalies with the most career wins

number of games won

Martin Brodeur, 1991–	Patrick Roy, 1984–2003	Ed Belfour, 1988–2007	Curtis Joseph, 1989–2009	Terry Sawchuck, 1945–1970
624	551	484	454	447

most valuable hockey team

Toronto Maple Leafs

The Toronto Maple Leafs are worth an astounding $505 million, making them the most valuable hockey team in the world. This value is determined by assigning a monetary value to each of the team's players, based on their skills, performance, and contract value. Formerly known as the Toronto Arenas, the team was formed in 1917. Ten years later, the team changed to its current name. The Leafs won 13 Stanley Cups between 1918 and 1967. Some of the most famous players associated with the team include Turk Broda, Tim Horton, Syl Apps, Darryl Sittler, and Ed Belfour. The team's home ice is at the Air Canada Centre.

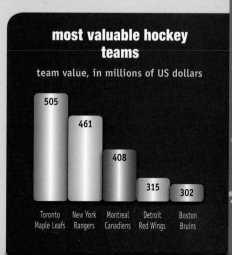

most valuable hockey teams

team value, in millions of US dollars

Toronto Maple Leafs	New York Rangers	Montreal Canadiens	Detroit Red Wings	Boston Bruins
505	461	408	315	302

skateboarder with the most x game gold medals

Tony Hawk

American Tony Hawk won ten gold medals for skateboarding in the Extreme Games between 1995 and 2002. All his medals came in vertical competition, meaning that the riders compete on a vert ramp similar to a half-pipe. Hawk is most famous for nailing the 900—completing 2.5 rotations in the air before landing back on the ramp. He has also invented many skateboarding tricks, including the McHawk, the Madonna, and the Stalefish. Although Hawk is retired from professional skateboarding, he is still active in several businesses, including video game consulting, film production, and clothing design.

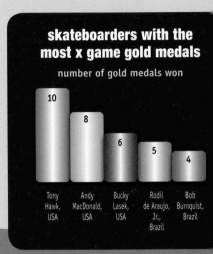

skateboarders with the most x game gold medals

number of gold medals won

Tony Hawk, USA	Andy MacDonald, USA	Bucky Lasek, USA	Rodil de Araujo, Jr., Brazil	Bob Burnquist, Brazil
10	8	6	5	4

athlete with the most x game medals

Dave Mirra

Dave Mirra has won 21 medals—14 gold, 4 silver, and 3 bronze—in X Game competition. He has medaled in every X Game since he entered the games in 1995. All of Mirra's medals have come in BMX competition, in which he performs tricks such as double backflips, front flips, triple tail whips, and backflip drop-ins. In 2006, Mirra formed his own bike company named Mirraco, and he now competes for the company with other top BMX riders. That same year marked Mirra's first absence from the X Games because of injury.

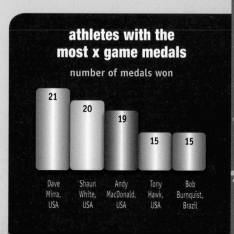

athletes with the most x game medals

number of medals won

Dave Mirra, USA	Shaun White, USA	Andy MacDonald, USA	Tony Hawk, USA	Bob Burnquist, Brazil
21	20	19	15	15

snowboarder with the most world championship medals

Nicolas Huet

Nicolas Huet has won five championship medals while competing as a snowboarder with the Fédération Internationale de Ski (FIS). Huet's medals include two golds, one silver, and two bronzes. Huet's first medal came in 1999 when he won gold in Germany, and his most recent medals came in 2005 when he won a silver and a bronze in Canada. His medals were earned on the parallel slalom and the parallel giant slalom. Called Nico, Huet spends his time golfing and surfing when he's not on the slopes.

snowboarders with the most world championship medals

number of medals won

Nicolas Huet, France	Antti Autti, Finland	Jasey-Jay Anderson, Canada	Seth Wescott, USA	Mike Jacoby, USA
5	4	4	4	3

science records

video games • internet
technology • vehicles

bestselling family video game

Wii Sports

Wii Sports sold 16.6 million copies worldwide in 2010. The game, which comes bundled with the Wii console, features five sports—tennis, bowling, golf, baseball, and boxing. Players use handheld controllers that respond to their body movements and mimic their actions on screen. Players can also create their own Mii caricatures in the game, and the Mii skill levels increase as players master the games. The game was first released in the United States in November 2006. Since then, Wii Sports has become one of the bestselling games of all time with 75.6 million units sold.

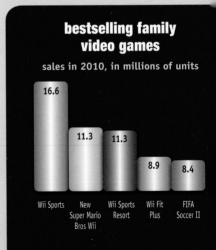

bestselling family video games

sales in 2010, in millions of units

Wii Sports	New Super Mario Bros Wii	Wii Sports Resort	Wii Fit Plus	FIFA Soccer II
16.6	11.3	11.3	8.9	8.4

bestselling video game console

Nintendo DS

The Nintendo DS was the bestselling video game console in 2010, with more than 1.32 million units sold. The handheld device features two screens, 3-D graphics, touch-screen technology, a microphone, and wireless connection. Other DS models include the DS Lite and the DSi. Together, the consoles have become the bestselling game platforms of all time with sales totaling 144.6 million units. There are hundreds of DS games available, including the popular Pokémon, Super Mario Bros., and Sonic the Hedgehog titles. The DS was first released in 2004.

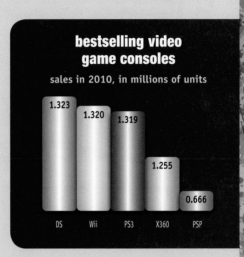

bestselling video game consoles

sales in 2010, in millions of units

DS	Wii	PS3	X360	PSP
1.323	1.320	1.319	1.255	0.666

fastest-selling family video game

Pokémon Diamond/Pearl

Pokémon Diamond/Pearl is the fastest-selling family video game in history, moving 3.49 million units worldwide in just one week of 2006. Since the game debuted, it has sold more than 17.7 million units across the globe. Published by Nintendo, the Pokémon brand follows a Pokémon trainer who is preparing for battle. Diamond and Pearl features 493 Pokémon, including all the species from previous games and new species introduced for the first time. Pokémon—a combination of the words "pocket" and "monster"—is one of the best-selling game franchises in history.

fastest-selling family video games

sales in one week, in millions of units

3.49	2.95	2.73	2.60	2.37
Pokémon Diamond/ Pearl	Pokémon Heart Gold/ Soul Silver	Super Smash Bros. Brawl	Pokémon Black/White	Mario Kart Wii

most-used e-mail service

Yahoo! Mail

Yahoo! Mail accounts for 3.1 percent of all Internet page visits per month—that's more than the next two most popular e-mail services combined. There are more than 274 million Yahoo! Mail users worldwide. Some popular features that the e-mail service includes are unlimited e-mail storage, instant and text messaging from mailboxes, and advanced protection from spam and viruses. The mail service, which is part of the bigger Yahoo! company, began in 1996. Founders David Filo and Jerry Yang created Yahoo! while they were students at Stanford University.

most-used e-mail services

percentage of visitor share per month

Yahoo! Mail	Windows Live Hotmail	Google Gmail	AOL E-mail	Comcast .net E-mail
3.10	1.03	1.00	0.51	0.37

most-visited website

Facebook

Facebook is the most popular site on the Internet, accounting for more than 10.48 percent of all page visits. The site has 500 million active users, and they spend about 700 billion minutes browsing the site each month. The average user has 130 friends and is connected to 80 different community pages, groups, or events. About 70 percent of Facebook users are outside the United States, and there are more than 70 different translations available on the site. The social networking site was developed by Mark Zuckerberg in 2004 as a way for Harvard students to communicate, but quickly spread to include anyone with computer access.

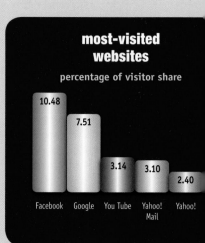

most-visited websites

percentage of visitor share

Facebook	Google	You Tube	Yahoo! Mail	Yahoo!
10.48	7.51	3.14	3.10	2.40

facebook

Facebook helps you connect and share with the people in your life.

Sign Up

It's free, and always will

First Name:

Last Name:

Your Email:

Re-enter Email:

New Password:

I am: Select Sex

Birthday: Month Day

Sign Up

English (US) Español Português (Brasil)

Books
Books
Kindle Books
Textbooks
Magazines

most-visited shopping site

Amazon.com

Shopping megasite Amazon.com has 50 million visitors browsing its products per month. The site, which got its start selling books, now offers everything from clothes and electronics to food and furniture. Amazon.com has formed alliances with other big-name companies, including Target, Toys "R" Us, and Borders. Founded by Jeffrey Bezos in 1994, it is headquartered in Seattle, Washington. The company also has separate websites in countries such as Japan, Canada, the United Kingdom, Germany, and France.

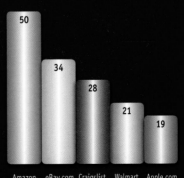

most-visited shopping sites

number of unique visitors per month, in millions

Amazon.com	eBay.com	Craigslist.com	Walmart.com	Apple.com
50	34	28	21	19

internet

most-visited search engine

Google

More than 63 percent of people browsing the Internet choose Google as their search engine. Google is the world's largest online index of websites. In addition, Google offers e-mail, maps, news, and financial services. Headquartered in California's Silicon Valley, the company runs more than one million servers and data center around the globe. Google was founded in 1998 by college students Larry Page and Sergey Brin. A "googol" is a 1 followed 100 zeros, and the site was named after the term to indicate its mission to organize the virtually infinite amount of information on the web.

most-visited search engines
percentage of visitor share

Google	Bing	Yahoo! Search	Ask	AOL Search
63.10	13.00	11.90	2.14	1.24

country with the most websites

Germany

There are 84.7 websites for every 1,000 people living in Germany. That means that there are about 7 million websites in the European country. Many websites originating from Germany end in ".de." There are more than 65.1 million Internet users in the country, which is about 79 percent of the population. That's the highest Internet usage in Europe. Germans aged 14 to 29 are the most likely to surf the web. The most popular websites in the country are very similar to those in the United States—they include Google, Facebook, YouTube, and eBay.

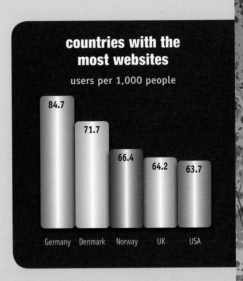

countries with the most websites

users per 1,000 people

Germany	Denmark	Norway	UK	USA
84.7	71.7	66.4	64.2	63.7

internet

country with the highest internet usage

Iceland

Iceland has the world's highest percentage of Internet users, with more than 97 percent of the country logging on to surf the web. That means about 301,600 people in the small European country have Internet access, and 97,900 are broadband subscribers. In comparison, only about 58 percent of the population in Europe as a whole goes online. Icelandic people mainly use the Internet to find information and to communicate, with about 45 percent of users also shopping online.

countries with the highes internet usage

percentage of population

Iceland	Norway	Sweden	Greenland	Saint Lucia
97.6	94.8	92.5	90.2	88.8

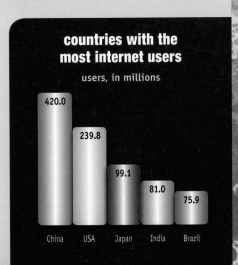

country with the most internet users

China

China dominates the world in Internet usage, with 420 million people—or about one-third of the country—browsing the World Wide Web under government censorship. The number of Internet users in China has tripled in the last five years. About 233 million Internet users browse from their cell phones. These phone surfers account for much of the increase in Internet users. People spend an average of almost 20 hours a week online. Some Internet activities that are becoming increasingly popular in China include banking and booking travel.

countries with the most internet users

users, in millions

China	USA	Japan	India	Brazil
420.0	239.8	99.1	81.0	75.9

bestselling cell phone brand

Nokia

Nokia is the most popular cell phone brand worldwide and accounted for 32.6 percent of the market share—or total number of people buying cell phones—in 2010. Since launching its first mobile phone in 1992, the Finnish company sold 453 million phones in 150 countries. Nokia introduced its first 3G phone in 2003, and went on to sell its 1 billionth phone in 2005. In 2007, Nokia's N95 became the first phone to combine GPS service and wireless broadband. The company operates 15 manufacturing plants across the globe, and employs 123,000 people.

bestselling cell phone brands

percentage of market share

Nokia	Samsung	LG Electronics	ZTE	Apple
32.6	20.2	8.4	3.7	3.4

Android

he Android maintains a slight lead in the country's smart phone race, with 29 percent f the market share. They are most popular vith buyers ages 18 to 34, and men slightly utnumber women in ownership rates. On verage, Android users have 22 apps. The op four apps of the Android are Google Maps, Facebook, the Weather Channel, and andora. And users remain loyal—more than '0 percent of current Android users intend to uy another when it comes time. More than 25 percent of all cell phone users now own a smart phone.

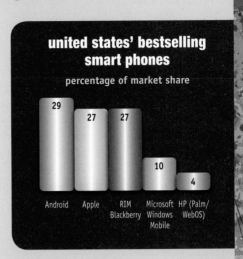

united states' bestselling smart phones

percentage of market share

Android	Apple	RIM Blackberry	Microsoft Windows Mobile	HP (Palm/ WebOS)
29	27	27	10	4

technology

country with the most cell phone accounts

United Arab Emirates

The United Arab Emirates has the highest percentage of cell phone users with 233 accounts per 100 people. With a small population of 4.6 million, there are 10.7 million cell phone accounts. This means that most people have more than one cell phone. It's common for countries such as the UAE—which has many foreign travelers—to have a high number of phones per person. This is because many travelers purchase a local cell phone to make calls within the country instead of trying to use their own from home. Cell phone use is most common in the large city of Dubai, which is the business and finance center of the country.

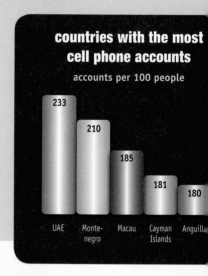

countries with the most cell phone accounts

accounts per 100 people

UAE	Monte-negro	Macau	Cayman Islands	Anguilla
233	210	185	181	180

country that watches the most tv

United States

The United States likes to watch a lot of television, averaging 38 hours of weekly program viewing per capita. That's the equivalent of almost 82 straight days, or 2.5 months per year. Some 98 percent of American households own at least one television, and about 54 percent of children have a set in their bedrooms. About 6 percent of families watch TV while eating dinner. About 70 percent of daycare centers use televisions as well. Each year, kids watch about 20,000 30-second commercials, which increases to 2 million by the time they are 65.

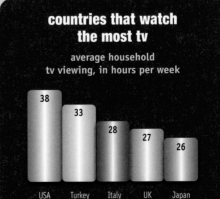

countries that watch the most tv

average household
tv viewing, in hours per week

USA	Turkey	Italy	UK	Japan
38	33	28	27	26

tallest roller coaster

Kingda Ka

Kingda Ka towers over Six Flags Great Adventure in Jackson, New Jersey, at a height of 456 feet (139 m). Its highest drop plummets riders down 418 feet (127 m). The steel coaster can reach a top speed of 128 miles (206 km) per hour in just 3.5 seconds, and it was the fastest coaster in the world when it opened in 2005. The entire 3,118-foot (950 m) ride is over in just 28 seconds. The hydraulic launch coaster is located in the Golden Kingdom section of the park. It can accommodate about 1,400 riders per hour.

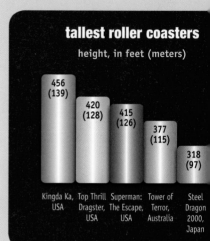

tallest roller coasters

height, in feet (meters)

Kingda Ka, USA	Top Thrill Dragster, USA	Superman: The Escape, USA	Tower of Terror, Australia	Steel Dragon 2000, Japan
456 (139)	420 (128)	415 (126)	377 (115)	318 (97)

fastest roller coaster

Formula Rossa

The Formula Rossa coaster in the United Arab Emirates speeds past the competition with a top speed of 149 miles (240 km) per hour. Located at Ferrari World in Dubai, riders climb into the F1 race car cockpits and can experience what 4.8 g-force actually feels like. The coaster's hydraulic launch system rockets the coaster to its top speed in just 4.9 seconds. The track is about 1.4 miles (2.2 km) long, with the sharpest turn measuring 70 degrees. To protect riders' eyes from flying insects, safety goggles must be worn throughout the ride.

fastest roller coasters

speed, in miles (kilometers) per hour

Formula Rossa, UAE	Kingda Ka, USA	Top Thrill Dragster, USA	Dodonpa, Japan	Steel Dragon 2000, Japan
149 (240)	128 (206)	120 (193)	106 (171)	95 (153)

largest cruise ships

Oasis of the Seas & Allure of the Seas

Royal Caribbean's sister cruise ships—*Oasis of the Seas* and *Allure of the Seas*—weigh in at 225,282 gross tons (228,897 t) each! These giant ships are more like floating cities with seven different themed neighborhoods: Central Park, Boardwalk, Royal Promenade, Pool and Sports Zone, Vitality at Sea Spa and Fitness Center, Entertainment Place, and Youth Zone. *Oasis of the Seas* and *Allure of the Seas* each span 16 decks and include more than 20 eateries, 3 pools, a water park, and a zip-line ride. Both ships have 2,700 staterooms and can accommodate a whopping 5,400 guests.

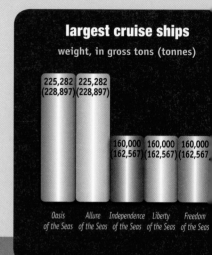

largest cruise ships

weight, in gross tons (tonnes)

Oasis of the Seas	Allure of the Seas	Independence of the Seas	Liberty of the Seas	Freedom of the Seas
225,282 (228,897)	225,282 (228,897)	160,000 (162,567)	160,000 (162,567)	160,000 (162,567)

fastest passenger train

CRH380AL

When China unveiled the CRH380AL commercial passenger train in 2010, it cruised into the record books with a top speed of 302 miles (486 km) per hour. The train reached its top speed in just 22 minutes. The train route connects Beijing and Shanghai, and will reduce the average travel time from 10 hours to 4 hours. The train is expected to carry about 80 million people along the 818-mile (1,316 km) route. The new train is part of China's $313 billion program to develop the world's most advanced train system by 2020.

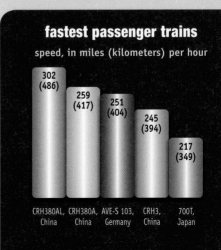

fastest passenger trains

speed, in miles (kilometers) per hour

CRH380AL, China	CRH380A, China	AVE-S 103, Germany	CRH3, China	700T, Japan
302 (486)	259 (417)	251 (404)	245 (394)	217 (349)

biggest monster truck

Bigfoot 5

The Bigfoot 5 truly is a monster—it measures 15.4 feet (4.7 m) high! That's about three times the height of an average car. Bigfoot 5 has 10-foot (3 m) Firestone Tundra tires, each weighing 2,400 pounds (1,088 kg), giving the truck a total weight of about 38,000 pounds (17,236 kg). The giant wheels were from an arctic snow train operated in Alaska by the US Army in the 1950s. This modified 1996 Ford F250 pickup truck is owned by Bob Chandler of St. Louis, Missouri. The great weight of this monster truck makes it too large to race.

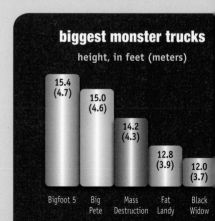

biggest monster trucks

height, in feet (meters)

Bigfoot 5	Big Pete	Mass Destruction	Fat Landy	Black Widow
15.4 (4.7)	15.0 (4.6)	14.2 (4.3)	12.8 (3.9)	12.0 (3.7)

smallest car

Peel P50

The Peel P50 is the smallest production car ever made, measuring just 4.25 feet (1.3 m) long. That's not much longer than the average adult bicycle! The Peel P50 was produced in the Isle of Man between 1962 and 1965, and only 46 cars were made. It is just big enough to hold one adult and one bag. The Peel P50 has three wheels, one door, one windshield wiper, and one headlight, and was available in red, white, or blue. The microcar weighs just 130 pounds (58.9 kg) and measures about 4 feet (1.2 m) tall. With its three-speed manual transmission, it can reach a top speed of 38 miles (61 km) an hour. However, it cannot go in reverse.

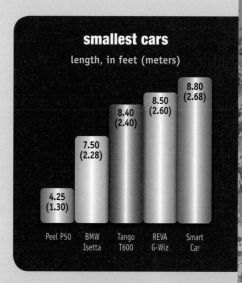

smallest cars

length, in feet (meters)

Peel P50	BMW Isetta	Tango T600	REVA G-Wiz	Smart Car
4.25 (1.30)	7.50 (2.28)	8.40 (2.40)	8.50 (2.60)	8.80 (2.68)

fastest land vehicle

Thrust SSC

The Thrust SSC, which stands for Supersonic Car, reached a speed of 763 miles (1,228 km) per hour on October 15, 1997. At that speed, a car could make it from San Francisco to New York City in less than four hours. The Thrust SSC is propelled by two jet engines capable of 110,000 horsepower. It has the same power as 1,000 Ford Escorts or 145 Formula One race cars. The Thrust SSC runs on jet fuel, using about 5 gallons (19 L) per second. It takes only approximately five seconds for this supersonic car to reach its top speed. It is 54 feet (16.5 m) long and weighs seven tons (6.4 t).

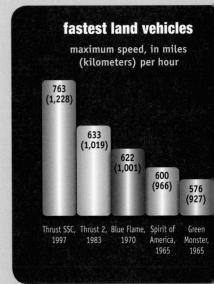

fastest land vehicles

maximum speed, in miles
(kilometers) per hour

763 (1,228)	633 (1,019)	622 (1,001)	600 (966)	576 (927)
Thrust SSC, 1997	Thrust 2, 1983	Blue Flame, 1970	Spirit of America, 1965	Green Monster, 1965

fastest production car

Bugatti Veyron 16.4 Super Sport

With a top cruising speed of 268 miles (431 km) per hour, the Bugatti Veyron 16.4 Super Sport is the fastest production car in the world. It can cruise at more than four times the average speed limit on most highways! The Super Sport has a sleek, aerodynamic design that feeds air to the 16-cylinder engine from the roof, rather than just above the hood. The shell of the car is made of carbon-fiber composites to make the car lighter, while maintaining its safety. The Super Sport debuted at the Pebble Beach Concourse in August 2010.

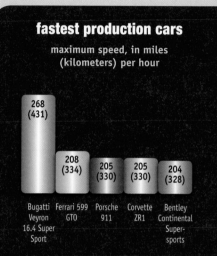

fastest production cars

maximum speed, in miles (kilometers) per hour

268 (431)	208 (334)	205 (330)	205 (330)	204 (328)
Bugatti Veyron 16.4 Super Sport	Ferrari 599 GTO	Porsche 911	Corvette ZR1	Bentley Continental Super-sports

fastest production motorcycle

Ducati Desmosedici RR

The Ducati Desmosedici RR can speed down the street at 196 miles (315 km) per hour. That's about three times the speed limit on most US highways! This Italian street bike, which was originally created to race in the MotoGP World Championships, can accelerate from 0 to 60 miles (96 km) per hour in just 2.43 seconds. The liquid-cooled, 16-valve engine has four cylinders with gear-driven crankshafts. The Desmosedici uses Bridgestone tires and Brembo brakes. Only 1,500 of these special bikes were created, and the base price for each is $72,500.

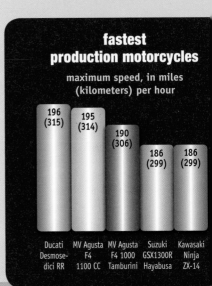

fastest production motorcycles

maximum speed, in miles (kilometers) per hour

Ducati Desmose-dici RR	MV Agusta F4 1100 CC	MV Agusta F4 1000 Tamburini	Suzuki GSX1300R Hayabusa	Kawasaki Ninja ZX-14
196 (315)	195 (314)	190 (306)	186 (299)	186 (299)

fastest traditional helicopter

Sikorsky X-2

The Sikorsky X-2 experimental compound helicopter reached a top speed of 287 miles (462 km) per hour in September 2010. The successful flight lasted just over one hour. Sikorsky was able to accomplish this record-breaking speed in 17 test flights with just over 16 flight hours. The company made several improvements to the original X-2—including reducing the drag, implementing rigid rotor blades, and finalizing vibration control—to achieve its success. Sikorsky continues to experiment with the X-2 to increase speed and performance for future models to be used by the military.

fastest traditional helicopters

maximum speed, in miles (kilometers) per hour

Sikorsky X-2	V-22 Osprey	G-LYNX	Euro-copter X3	Sikorsky S76C
287 (462)	275 (443)	249 (401)	207 (333)	177 (285)

lightest jet

BD-5J Microjet

The BD-5J Microjet weighs only 358.8 pounds (162.7 kg), making it the lightest jet in the world. At only 12 feet (3.7 m) in length, it is one of the smallest as well. This tiny jet has a height of 5.6 feet (1.7 m) and a wingspan of 17 feet (5.2 m). The Microjet uses a TRS-18 turbojet engine. It can reach a top speed of 320 miles (514.9 km) per hour, but can carry only 32 gallons (121 L) of fuel at a time. A new BD-5J costs around $200,000. This high-tech gadget was flown by James Bond in the movie *Octopussy*, and it is also occasionally used by the US military.

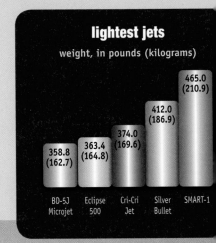

lightest jets

weight, in pounds (kilograms)

BD-5J Microjet	Eclipse 500	Cri-Cri Jet	Silver Bullet	SMART-1
358.8 (162.7)	363.4 (164.8)	374.0 (169.6)	412.0 (186.9)	465.0 (210.9)

fastest plane

X-43A

NASA's experimental X-43A plane reached a top speed of Mach 9.8—or more than nine times the speed of sound—on a test flight over the Pacific Ocean in November 2004. The X-43A was mounted on top of a Pegasus rocket booster and was carried into the sky by a B-52 aircraft. The booster was then fired, taking the X-43A about 110,000 feet (33,530 m) above the ground. The rocket was detached from the unmanned X-43A, and the plane flew unassisted for several minutes. At this rate of 7,459 miles (12,004 km) per hour, a plane could circle Earth in just over three and a half hours!

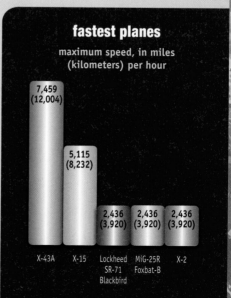

fastest planes

maximum speed, in miles (kilometers) per hour

7,459 (12,004)	5,115 (8,232)	2,436 (3,920)	2,436 (3,920)	2,436 (3,920)
X-43A	X-15	Lockheed SR-71 Blackbird	MiG-25R Foxbat-B	X-2

nature records

natural formations • animals • weather
plants • disasters • environment

largest diamond

Golden Jubilee

The Golden Jubilee is the world's largest faceted diamond, with a weight of 545.67 carats. This gigantic gem got its name when it was presented to the king of Thailand in 1997 for the Golden Jubilee—or 50th anniversary celebration—of his reign. The diamond weighed 755.5 carats when it was discovered in a South African mine in 1986. Once it was cut, the diamond featured 148 perfectly symmetrical facets. The process took almost a year because of the diamond's size and multiple tension points. The diamond is on display at the Royal Museum of Bangkok in Thailand.

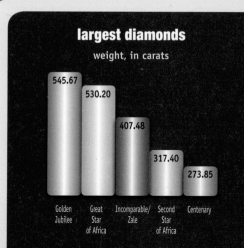

largest diamonds

weight, in carats

545.67	530.20	407.48	317.40	273.85
Golden Jubilee	Great Star of Africa	Incomparable/ Zale	Second Star of Africa	Centenary

tallest mountain

Mount Everest

Mount Everest's tallest peak towers 29,035 feet (8,850 m) into the air, and it is the highest point on Earth. This peak is an unbelievable 5.5 miles (8.8 km) above sea level. Mount Everest is located in the Himalayas, on the border between Nepal and Tibet. The mountain got its official name from surveyor Sir George Everest. In 1953, Sir Edmund Hillary and Tenzing Norgay were the first people to reach the peak. In 2008, the Olympic torch was carried up to the top of the mountain on its way to the games in Beijing.

tallest mountains

highest point, in feet (meters)

Mount Everest, Asia	K2, Asia	Kangchen-junga, Asia	Lhotse, Asia	Makalu, Asia
29,035 (8,850)	28,250 (8,611)	28,169 (8,586)	27,940 (8,516)	27,766 (8,463)

tallest volcano

Ojos del Salado

Located on the border between Argentina and Chile, Ojos del Salado towers 22,595 feet (6,887 m) above the surrounding Atacama Desert. It is the second-highest peak in the Andean mountain chain. Ojos del Salado is a composite volcano, which means that it is a tall, symmetrical cone that was built by layers of lava flow, ash, and cinder. There is no record of the volcano erupting, but this could be because of the volcano's remote location. Ojos del Salado is a very popular spot for mountain climbing.

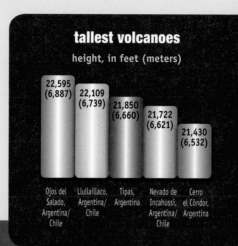

tallest volcanoes

height, in feet (meters)

22,595 (6,887)	22,109 (6,739)	21,850 (6,660)	21,722 (6,621)	21,430 (6,532)
Ojos del Salado, Argentina/ Chile	Llullaillaco, Argentina/ Chile	Tipas, Argentina	Nevado de Incahussi, Argentina/ Chile	Cerro el Cóndor, Argentina

natural formations

natural formations

largest lake

Caspian Sea

This giant inland body of salt water stretches for almost 750 miles (1,207 km) from north to south, with an average width of about 200 miles (322 km). Altogether, it covers 143,200 square miles (370,901 sq km). The Caspian Sea is located east of the Caucasus Mountains in central Asia. It is bordered by Iran, Russia, Kazakhstan, Azerbaijan, and Turkmenistan. The Caspian Sea has an average depth of about 550 feet (170 m). It is an important fishing resource, with species including sturgeon, salmon, perch, herring, and carp. Other animals living in the Caspian Sea include porpoises, seals, and tortoises. The sea is estimated to be 30 million years old and became landlocked 5.5 million years ago.

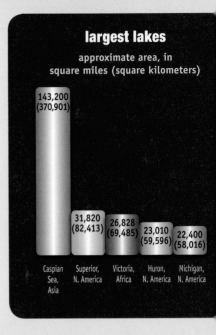

largest lakes

approximate area, in square miles (square kilometers)

Caspian Sea, Asia	143,200 (370,901)
Superior, N. America	31,820 (82,413)
Victoria, Africa	26,828 (69,485)
Huron, N. America	23,010 (59,596)
Michigan, N. America	22,400 (58,016)

largest desert

Sahara

Located in northern Africa, the Sahara Desert covers approximately 3.5 million square miles (9.1 million sq km). It stretches for 5,200 miles (8,372 km) through the countries of Morocco, Algeria, Tunisia, Libya, Egypt, Mauritania, Mali, Niger, Chad, and Sudan. The Sahara gets very little rainfall—less than 8 inches (20 cm) per year. Even with its harsh environment, some 2.5 million people—mostly nomads—call the Sahara home. Date palms and acacias grow near oases. Some of the animals that live in the Sahara include gazelles, antelopes, jackals, foxes, and badgers.

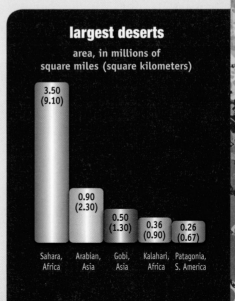

largest deserts

area, in millions of
square miles (square kilometers)

Desert	Area
Sahara, Africa	3.50 (9.10)
Arabian, Asia	0.90 (2.30)
Gobi, Asia	0.50 (1.30)
Kalahari, Africa	0.36 (0.90)
Patagonia, S. America	0.26 (0.67)

longest river

Nile

The Nile River in Africa stretches 4,145 miles (6,671 km) from the tributaries of Lake Victoria in Tanzania and Uganda out to the Mediterranean Sea. Because of varying depths, boats can sail on only about 2,000 miles (3,217 km) of the river. The Nile flows through Rwanda, Uganda, Sudan, and Egypt. The river's water supply is crucial to the existence of these African countries. The Nile's precious water is used to irrigate crops and to generate electricity. The Aswan Dam and the Aswan High Dam—both located in Egypt—are used to store the autumn floodwater for later use. The Nile is also used to transport goods from city to city along the river.

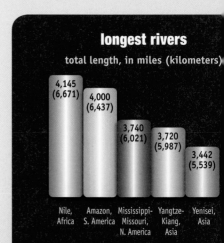

longest rivers

total length, in miles (kilometers)

Nile, Africa	4,145 (6,671)
Amazon, S. America	4,000 (6,437)
Mississippi-Missouri, N. America	3,740 (6,021)
Yangtze-Kiang, Asia	3,720 (5,987)
Yenisei, Asia	3,442 (5,539)

Pacific

The Pacific Ocean covers almost 64 million square miles (166 million sq km) and reaches 36,200 feet (11,000 m) below sea level at its greatest depth—the Mariana Trench (near the Philippines). In fact, this ocean is so large that it covers about one-third of the planet (more than all of Earth's land put together) and holds more than half of all the seawater on Earth. The United States could fit inside this ocean 18 times! Some of the major bodies of water included in the Pacific are the Bering Sea, the Coral Sea, the Philippine Sea, and the Gulf of Alaska.

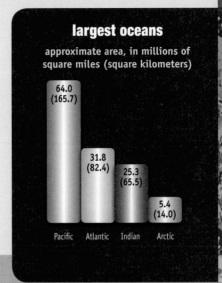

largest oceans

approximate area, in millions of square miles (square kilometers)

Pacific	Atlantic	Indian	Arctic
64.0 (165.7)	31.8 (82.4)	25.3 (65.5)	5.4 (14.0)

natural formations

largest island

Greenland

Located in the North Atlantic Ocean, Greenland covers more than 840,000 square miles (2,175,600 sq km). Not including continents, it is the largest island in the world. Its jagged coastline is approximately 24,400 miles (39,267 km) long—about the same distance as Earth's circumference at the equator. Mountain chains are located on Greenland's east and west coasts, and the coastline is indented by fjords, or thin bodies of water bordered by steep cliffs. From north to south, the island stretches for about 1,660 miles (2,670 km). About 700,000 square miles (1,813,000 sq km) of this massive island are covered by a giant ice sheet. The island also contains the world's largest national park—Northeast Greenland National Park—with an area of 375,291 square miles (972,000 sq km).

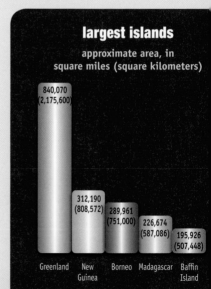

largest islands

approximate area, in square miles (square kilometers)

Greenland	840,070 (2,175,600)
New Guinea	312,190 (808,572)
Borneo	289,961 (751,000)
Madagascar	226,674 (587,086)
Baffin Island	195,926 (507,448)

largest crustacean

Giant Spider Crab

The giant spider crab has a 12-foot (3.7 m) leg span. That's almost wide enough to take up two parking spaces! The crab's body measures about 15 inches (38.1 cm) wide. Its ten long legs are jointed, and the first pair has large claws at the end. The giant sea creature can weigh 35–44 pounds (16–20 kg). It feeds on dead animals and shellfish it finds on the ocean floor. Giant spider crabs live in the deep water of the Pacific Ocean off southern Japan.

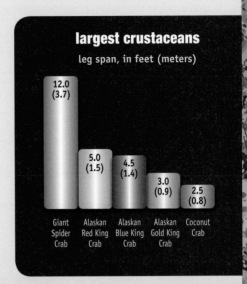

largest crustaceans

leg span, in feet (meters)

12.0 (3.7)	5.0 (1.5)	4.5 (1.4)	3.0 (0.9)	2.5 (0.8)
Giant Spider Crab	Alaskan Red King Crab	Alaskan Blue King Crab	Alaskan Gold King Crab	Coconut Crab

animals

largest cephalopod

Colossal Squid

Living up to 6,000 (1,829 m) feet deep in the Antarctic Ocean, the colossal squid can grow to a length of 46 feet (14 m). That's about the same size as three SUVs! The squid, which is very rarely seen by people, can weigh about 1,500 pounds (681 kg). Its eyes are the size of dinner plates, and are the largest eyes in the animal kingdom. The colossal squid uses its 20-foot (6 m) long tentacles to catch its prey. In addition to the two tentacles, the giant cephalopod has eight arms. In the center of its body, the squid has a razor-sharp beak that it uses to shred its prey before eating it.

largest cephalopods
size, in feet (meters)

Colossal Squid	Giant Squid	Bigfin Squid	North Pacific Giant Octopus	Glass Squid
46 (14)	43 (13)	26 (8)	16 (5)	10 (3)

biggest fish

Whale Shark

Although the average length of a whale shark is 30 feet (9 m), many have been known to reach up to 60 feet (18 m) long. That's the same length as two school buses! Whale sharks also weigh an average of 50,000 pounds (22,680 kg). As with most sharks, the females are larger than the males. Their mouths measure about 5 feet (1.5 m) long and contain about 3,000 teeth. Amazingly, these gigantic fish eat only microscopic plankton and tiny fish. They float near the surface looking for food.

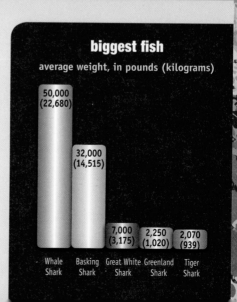

biggest fish

average weight, in pounds (kilograms)

Whale Shark	Basking Shark	Great White Shark	Greenland Shark	Tiger Shark
50,000 (22,680)	32,000 (14,515)	7,000 (3,175)	2,250 (1,020)	2,070 (939)

animals

Great White

With a total of 249 known unprovoked attacks on humans, great white sharks are the most dangerous predators in the sea. A great white can measure more than 20 feet (6.1 m) in length and weigh up to 3,800 pounds (1,723 kg). Because of the sharks' size, they can feed on large prey, including seals, dolphins, and even small whales. Often, when a human is attacked by a great white, it is because the shark has mistaken the person for its typical prey. The sharks make their homes in most waters throughout the world, but are most frequently found off the coasts of Australia, South Africa, California, and Mexico.

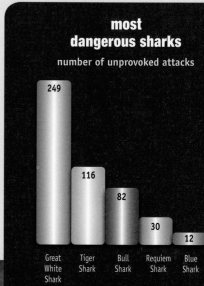

most dangerous sharks

number of unprovoked attacks

Great White Shark	Tiger Shark	Bull Shark	Requiem Shark	Blue Shark
249	116	82	30	12

biggest dolphin

Orca

The orca is actually a member of the dolphin family and can measure up to 32 feet (9.7 m) in length and weigh up to 6 tons (5.4 t). These powerful marine mammals are carnivores with 4-inch (1.6 cm) long teeth, and they feed mainly on seals, sea lions, and smaller whales. Orcas live in pods of up to 40 other whales, and pod members help one another round up prey. Killer whales can live for up to 80 years. They are also very intelligent, and orcas in captivity have worked with trainers in aquariums to perform in shows.

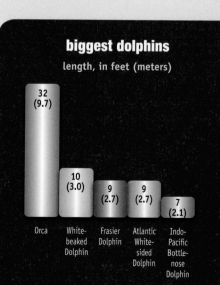

biggest dolphins

length, in feet (meters)

Orca	White-beaked Dolphin	Frasier Dolphin	Atlantic White-sided Dolphin	Indo-Pacific Bottle-nose Dolphin
32 (9.7)	10 (3.0)	9 (2.7)	9 (2.7)	7 (2.1)

fastest fish

Sailfish

A sailfish once grabbed a fishing line and dragged it 300 feet (91 m) away in just three seconds. That means it was swimming at an average speed of 69 miles (109 km) per hour—higher than the average speed limit on a highway! Sailfish are very large—they average 6 feet (1.8 m) long, but can grow up to 11 feet (3.4 m). Sailfish eat squid and surface-dwelling fish. Sometimes several sailfish will work together to catch their prey. They are found in both the Atlantic and Pacific oceans and prefer a water temperature of about 80°F (27°C).

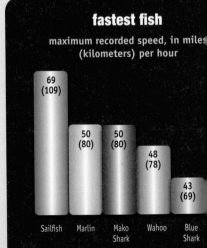

fastest fish

maximum recorded speed, in miles (kilometers) per hour

Sailfish	Marlin	Mako Shark	Wahoo	Blue Shark
69 (109)	50 (80)	50 (80)	48 (78)	43 (69)

fastest shark

Mako Shark

A mako shark can cruise through the water at 50 miles (79.4 km) per hour. This super speed helps the shark catch its food, which consists mostly of tuna, herring, mackerel, swordfish, and porpoise. Occasionally makos even build up enough speed to leap out of the water. Mako sharks average 7 feet (2.1 m) in length, but can grow up to 12 feet (3.7 m) and weigh on average 1,000 pounds (454 kg). These sharks are found in temperate and tropical seas throughout the world.

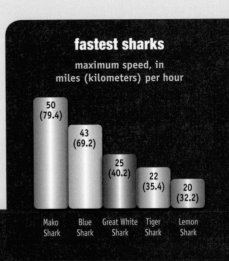

fastest sharks

maximum speed, in miles (kilometers) per hour

Mako Shark	Blue Shark	Great White Shark	Tiger Shark	Lemon Shark
50 (79.4)	43 (69.2)	25 (40.2)	22 (35.4)	20 (32.2)

heaviest marine mammal

Blue Whale

Blue whales are the largest animals that have ever inhabited Earth. They can weigh more than 143.3 tons (130 t) and measure over 100 feet (30 m) long. Amazingly, these gentle giants only eat krill—small, shrimplike animals. A blue whale can eat about 4 tons (3.6 t) of krill each day in the summer, when food is plentiful. To catch the krill, a whale gulps as much as 17,000 gallons (64,600 L) of seawater into its mouth at one time. Then it uses its tongue—which can be as big as a car—to push the water back out. The krill get caught in hairs on the whale's baleen (a keratin structure that hangs down from the roof of the whale's mouth).

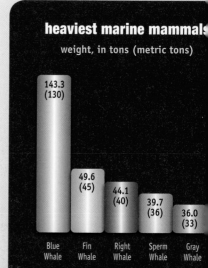

heaviest marine mammals

weight, in tons (metric tons)

Blue Whale	Fin Whale	Right Whale	Sperm Whale	Gray Whale
143.3 (130)	49.6 (45)	44.1 (40)	39.7 (36)	36.0 (33)

Sperm Whale

The sperm whale's brain is the largest animal brain in the world, weighing more than 17 pounds (7.7 kg). That's more than five times the size of a human brain. Sperm whales can grow to about 60 feet (18 m) long and weigh up to 45 tons (41 t). The head makes up about one-third of the animal's body. Sperm whales can also dive deeper than any other whale, reaching depths of 3,300 feet (1,006 m) in search of squid. They can eat about 1 ton (0.9 t) of fish and squid daily. Sperm whales can be found in all oceans, and they generally live in pods of about a dozen adults and their offspring.

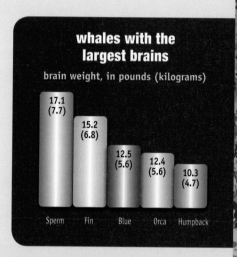

whales with the largest brains

brain weight, in pounds (kilograms)

Sperm	Fin	Blue	Orca	Humpback
17.1 (7.7)	15.2 (6.8)	12.5 (5.6)	12.4 (5.6)	10.3 (4.7)

largest bird wingspan

Marabou Stork

With a wingspan that can reach up to 13 feet (4 m), the marabou stork has the largest wingspan of any bird. These large storks weigh up to 20 pounds (9 kg) and can grow up to 5 feet (150 cm) tall. Their long leg and toe bones are actually hollow. This adaptation is very important for flight because it makes the bird lighter. Although marabous eat insects, small mammals, and fish, the majority of their food is carrion—meat that is already dead. In fact, the stork's head and neck do not have any feathers. This helps the bird stay clean as it sticks its head into carcasses to pick out scraps of food.

largest bird wingspans

wingspan, in feet (meters)

13 (4.0)	12 (3.7)	11 (3.4)	10 (3.0)	10 (3.0)
Marabou Stork	Albatross	Trumpeter Swan	Mute Swan	Whooper Swan

biggest penguin

Emperor Penguin

Emperor penguins are giants among their species, growing to a height of 44 inches (111.7 cm) and weighing up to 80 pounds (37 kg). These penguins are the only animals that spend the entire winter on the open ice in Antarctica, withstanding temperatures of up to -75°F (-60°C). The female penguin lays a 1-pound (0.5 kg) egg on the ice, and then goes off to hunt for weeks at a time. The male penguin scoops up the egg, and keeps it warm on his feet below his toasty belly. When the eggs hatch, the females return with food.

biggest penguins
height in inches (centimeters)

Emperor Penguin	King Penguin	Gentoo Penguin	Yellow-eyed Penguin	Chinstrap Penguin
44 (111.7)	37 (93.9)	35 (88.9)	31 (78.7)	30 (76.2)

longest bird migration

Arctic Tern

The arctic tern migrates from Maine to the coast of Africa, and then on to Antarctica, flying some 22,000 miles (35,406 km) a year. That's almost the same distance as the Earth's circumference. Some don't complete the journey, however—young terns fly the first half of the journey with their parents, but remain in the Antarctic for a year or two. When they have matured, the birds fly back to Maine and the surrounding areas. Scientists are puzzled about how these birds remember the way back after only making the journey once, so early in their lives.

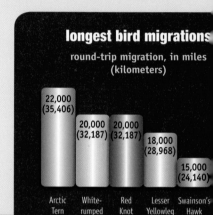

longest bird migrations

round-trip migration, in miles (kilometers)

Arctic Tern	White-rumped Sandpiper	Red Knot	Lesser Yellowleg	Swainson's Hawk
22,000 (35,406)	20,000 (32,187)	20,000 (32,187)	18,000 (28,968)	15,000 (24,140)

bird that builds the largest nest

Bald Eagle

With a nest that can measure 8 feet (2.4 m) wide and 16 feet (4.9 m) deep, bald eagles have plenty of room to move around. These birds of prey have wingspans of up to 7.5 feet (2.3 m) and need a home that they can nest in comfortably. By carefully constructing their nest with sticks, branches, and plant material, a pair of bald eagles can balance their home—which can weigh up to 4,000 pounds (1,814 kg)—on the top of a tree or cliff. These nests are usually located by rivers or coastlines, the birds' watery hunting grounds. Called an aerie, this home will be used for the rest of the eagles' lives.

birds that build the largest nests

nest diameter, in feet (meters)

Bald Eagle	Sociable Weaver	Maguari Stork	Great Blue Heron	Monk Parakeet
8.0 (2.4)	7.0 (2.1)	6.0 (1.8)	4.5 (1.4)	3.0 (0.9)

largest bird egg

Ostrich Egg

Ostriches—the world's largest birds—can lay eggs that measure 5 inches by 6 inches (13 cm by 16 cm) and weigh up to 4 pounds (1.8 kg). In fact, just one ostrich egg weighs as much as 24 chicken eggs. The egg yolk makes up one-third of the volume. Although the eggshell is only 0.08 inches (2 mm) thick, it is tough enough to withstand the weight of a 345-pound (157 kg) ostrich. An ostrich hen can lay from 10 to 70 eggs each year. Females are usually able to recognize their own eggs, even when they are mixed in with those of other females in their shared nest.

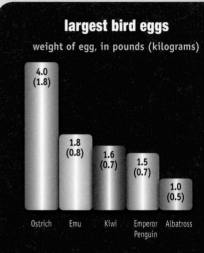

largest bird eggs

weight of egg, in pounds (kilograms)

Ostrich	Emu	Kiwi	Emperor Penguin	Albatross
4.0 (1.8)	1.8 (0.8)	1.6 (0.7)	1.5 (0.7)	1.0 (0.5)

California condor

most endangered US animal group

Birds

There are 77 different species of birds that are on the endangered list in the United States. For a bird to qualify for the endangered species list, it must be in danger of extinction in all or most of its habitat. Some of the most endangered bird species are the crested shelduck, the swallow-tailed kite, and the California condor. Several bird species that have previously been on the endangered species list—such as the peregrine falcon and the American bald eagle—have made successful comebacks, and their populations are now stable. Many more species, however, have gone from endangered to extinct.

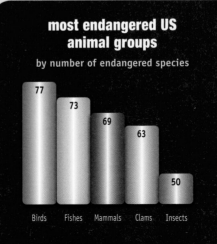

most endangered US animal groups

by number of endangered species

Birds	Fishes	Mammals	Clams	Insects
77	73	69	63	50

biggest bear

Polar Bear

A massive male polar bear can weigh in at up to 1,600 pounds (726 kg), which is about the same weight as ten grown men. Females are smaller than the males, and the weight of both genders fluctuates when food is scarce. The 8-foot (2.4 m) tall animals live in the frigid Arctic, patrolling the ice and surrounding water for food. Polar bears are excellent swimmers, and can travel more than 100 miles (161 km) in icy water searching for seals to eat. Their dense coats protect them from snow, ice, and wind. They even have thick strips of fur on their paws to insulate their feet and help them grip the ice.

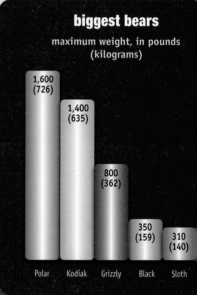

biggest bears
maximum weight, in pounds (kilograms)

Polar	Kodiak	Grizzly	Black	Sloth
1,600 (726)	1,400 (635)	800 (362)	350 (159)	310 (140)

heaviest land mammal

African Elephant

Weighing in at up to 14,430 pounds (6,545 kg) and measuring approximately 24 feet (7.3 m) long, African elephants are truly humongous. Even at their great size, they are strictly vegetarian. They will, however, eat up to 500 pounds (226 kg) of vegetation a day! Their two tusks—which are actually elongated teeth—grow continuously during their lives and can reach about 9 feet (2.7 m) in length. Elephants live in small groups of 8 to 15 family members with one female (called a cow) as the leader.

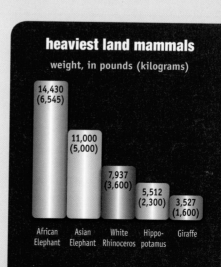

heaviest land mammals
weight, in pounds (kilograms)

African Elephant	14,430 (6,545)
Asian Elephant	11,000 (5,000)
White Rhinoceros	7,937 (3,600)
Hippopotamus	5,512 (2,300)
Giraffe	3,527 (1,600)

animals

largest rodent

Capybara

Capybaras reach an average length of 4 feet (1.2 m), stand about 20 inches (51 cm) tall, and weigh 75–150 pounds (34–68 kg)! That's about the same size as a Labrador retriever. Also known as water hogs and carpinchos, capybaras are found in South and Central America, where they spend much of their time in groups, looking for food. They are strictly vegetarian and have been known to raid gardens for melons and squash. Their partially webbed feet make capybaras excellent swimmers. They can dive down to the bottom of a lake or river to find plants and stay there for up to five minutes.

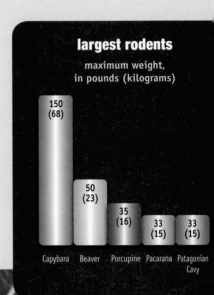

largest rodents
maximum weight,
in pounds (kilograms)

Capybara	Beaver	Porcupine	Pacarana	Patagonian Cavy
150 (68)	50 (23)	35 (16)	33 (15)	33 (15)

biggest wolf

Arctic Wolf

The gray wolf is the largest member of the Canidae family, which also includes foxes, coyotes, jackals, and dogs. There are five subspecies of the gray wolf, and of them, the Arctic wolf is the largest. Measuring 32 inches (81 cm) long and weighing up to 175 pounds (79 kg), these meat-eating mammals live and hunt in packs. Working together, they can take down prey much larger than themselves, including deer, moose, and caribou. Gray wolves can chase prey for more than 20 minutes, sometimes reaching speeds of 35 miles (56 km) per hour. They live throughout North America and in parts of Europe and Asia.

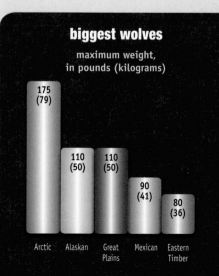

biggest wolves

maximum weight,
in pounds (kilograms)

Arctic	Alaskan	Great Plains	Mexican	Eastern Timber
175 (79)	110 (50)	110 (50)	90 (41)	80 (36)

fastest land mammal

Cheetah

For short spurts, these sleek mammals can reach a speed of 65 miles (105 km) per hour. They can accelerate from 0 to 40 miles (64 km) per hour in just three strides. Their quickness easily enables these large African cats to outrun their prey. All other African cats can only stalk their prey because they lack the cheetah's amazing speed. Unlike the paws of all other cats, cheetah paws do not have skin sheaths (thin protective coverings). Their claws, therefore, cannot be retracted.

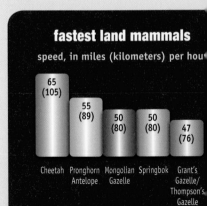

fastest land mammals

speed, in miles (kilometers) per hour

65 (105)	55 (89)	50 (80)	50 (80)	47 (76)
Cheetah	Pronghorn Antelope	Mongolian Gazelle	Springbok	Grant's Gazelle/ Thompson's Gazelle

tallest land animal

Giraffe

Giraffes are the giants among mammals, growing up to 18 feet (5.5 m) in height. That means an average giraffe could look through the window of a two-story building. A giraffe's neck is 18 times longer than a human's, but both mammals have exactly the same number of neck bones. A giraffe's long legs enable it to outrun most of its enemies. When cornered, a giraffe has been known to kill a lion with a single kick to the head.

some of the tallest land animals

height, in feet (meters)

18.0 (5.5)	7.0 (2.1)	6.5 (2.0)	6.0 (1.8)	5.0 (1.5)
Giraffe	African Elephant	Camel	Moose	Rhinoceros

largest bat

Giant Flying Fox

The giant flying fox—a member of the megabat family—can have a wingspan of up to 6 feet (1.8 m). These furry mammals average just 7 wing beats per second, but can travel more than 40 miles (64 km) a night in search of food. Unlike smaller bats, which use echolocation, flying foxes rely on their acute vision and sense of smell to locate fruit, pollen, and nectar. Flying foxes got their name because their faces resemble a fox's face. Megabats live in the tropical areas of Africa, Asia, and Australia.

largest bats

wingspan, in feet (meters)

Giant Flying Fox	Malayan Flying Fox	Golden Crown	Lyle's Flying Fox	Indian Flying Fox
6.0 (1.8)	5.7 (1.7)	5.5 (1.6)	5.0 (1.5)	4.4 (1.3)

Gorilla

Gorillas are the kings of the primate family, weighing in at up to 400 pounds (181 kg). The eastern lowland gorilla is the largest of the four subspecies of gorillas, which also include western lowland, Cross River, and mountain. All gorillas are found in Africa, and all but mountain gorillas live in tropical forests. They are mostly plant eaters, but will occasionally eat small animals. An adult male gorilla can eat up to 45 pounds (32 kg) of food in a day. Gorillas live in groups of about 4 to 12 family members, and can live for about 35 years in the wild.

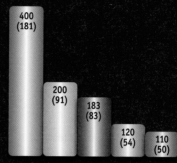

largest primates

maximum weight,
in pounds (kilograms)

Gorilla	Orangutan	Human	Chimpan-zee	Bonobo
400 (181)	200 (91)	183 (83)	120 (54)	110 (50)

deadliest amphibian

Poison Dart Frog

Poison dart frogs are found mostly in the tropical rain forests of Central and South America, where they live on the moist land. These lethal amphibians have enough poison to kill up to 20 humans. A dart frog's poison is so effective that native Central and South Americans sometimes coat their hunting arrows or hunting darts with it. These brightly colored frogs can be yellow, orange, red, green, blue, or any combination of these colors. They measure only 0.5–2 inches (1–5 cm) long. There are approximately 75 different species of poison dart frogs.

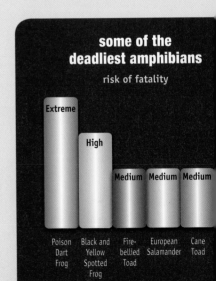

some of the deadliest amphibians

risk of fatality

Poison Dart Frog	Black and Yellow Spotted Frog	Fire-bellied Toad	European Salamander	Cane Toad
Extreme	High	Medium	Medium	Medium

Reticulated Python

Some adult reticulated pythons can grow to 27 feet (8.2 m) long, but most reach an average length of 17 feet (5 m). That's almost the length of an average school bus! These pythons live mostly in Asia, from Myanmar to Indonesia to the Philippines. The python has teeth that curve backward to hold its prey still. It hunts mainly at night and will eat mammals and birds. Reticulated pythons are slow-moving creatures that kill their prey by constriction, or strangulation.

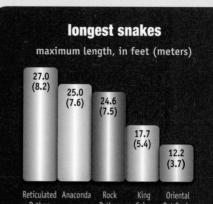

longest snakes

maximum length, in feet (meters)

Reticulated Python	Anaconda	Rock Python	King Cobra	Oriental Rat Snake
27.0 (8.2)	25.0 (7.6)	24.6 (7.5)	17.7 (5.4)	12.2 (3.7)

snake with the longest fangs

Gaboon Viper

The fangs of a Gaboon viper measure 2 inches (5.1 cm) in length! These giant fangs fold up against the snake's mouth so it does not pierce its own skin. When it is ready to strike its prey, the fangs snap down into position. The snake can grow up to 7 feet (2 m) long and weigh 18 pounds (8 kg). It is found in Africa and is perfectly camouflaged for hunting on the ground beneath leaves and grasses. The Gaboon viper's poison is not as toxic as some other snakes', but it is quite dangerous because of the amount of poison it can inject at one time. The snake is not very aggressive, however, and usually attacks only when bothered.

snakes with the longest fangs

fang length, in inches (centimeters)

Gaboon Viper	Bush-master	Black Mamba	Diamond-back Rattlesnake	Australian Taipan
2.0 (5.1)	1.5 (3.8)	1.0 (2.5)	1.0 (2.5)	0.7 (1.8)

deadliest snake

Black Mamba

With just one bite, an African black mamba snake releases a venom powerful enough to kill up to 200 humans. A bite from this snake is almost always fatal if it is not treated immediately. This large member of the cobra family grows to about 14 feet (4.3 m) long. In addition to its deadly poison, it is a very aggressive snake. It will raise its body off the ground when it feels threatened. It then spreads its hood and strikes swiftly at its prey with its long front teeth. A black mamba is also very fast—it can move along at about 7 miles (11.7 km) per hour for short bursts.

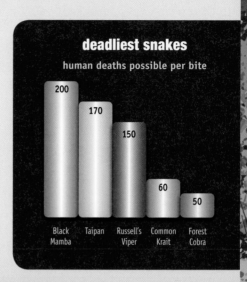

deadliest snakes

human deaths possible per bite

Black Mamba	Taipan	Russell's Viper	Common Krait	Forest Cobra
200	170	150	60	50

largest amphibian

Chinese Giant Salamander

With a length of 6 feet (1.8 m) and a weight of 55 pounds (25 kg), Chinese giant salamanders rule the amphibian world. This salamander has a large head, but its eyes and nostrils are small. It has short legs, a long tail, and very smooth skin. This large creature can be found in the streams of northeastern, central, and southern China. It feeds on fish, frogs, crabs, and snakes. The Chinese giant salamander will not hunt its prey. It will wait until a potential meal wanders too close and then grab it in its mouth. Because many people enjoy the taste of the salamander's meat, it is often hunted and its population is shrinking.

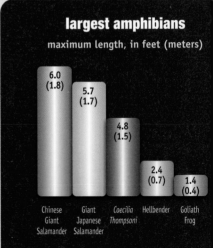

largest amphibians

maximum length, in feet (meters)

Chinese Giant Salamander	Giant Japanese Salamander	*Caecilia Thompsoni*	Hellbender	Goliath Frog
6.0 (1.8)	5.7 (1.7)	4.8 (1.5)	2.4 (0.7)	1.4 (0.4)

largest frog

Goliath Frog

The Goliath frog has a body that measures 13 inches (33 cm) long, but when its legs are extended, its total body length can increase to more than 2.5 feet (0.76 m). These gigantic frogs can weigh around 7 pounds (3 kg). Oddly enough, the eggs and tadpoles of this species are the same size as smaller frogs'. Goliath frogs are found only in the western African countries of Equatorial Guinea and Cameroon. They live in rivers that are surrounded by dense rain forests. These huge amphibians are becoming endangered, mostly because their rain forest homes are being destroyed.

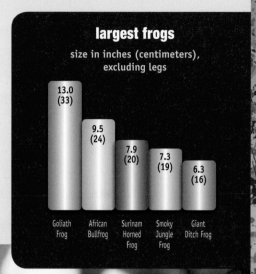

largest frogs
size in inches (centimeters), excluding legs

Goliath Frog	African Bullfrog	Surinam Horned Frog	Smoky Jungle Frog	Giant Ditch Frog
13.0 (33)	9.5 (24)	7.9 (20)	7.3 (19)	6.3 (16)

largest lizard

Komodo Dragon

With a length of 10 feet (3 m) and a weight of 300 pounds (136 kg), Komodo dragons are the largest lizards roaming the earth. A Komodo dragon has a long neck and tail, and strong legs. These members of the monitor family are found mainly on Komodo Island, located in the Lesser Sunda Islands of Indonesia. Komodos are dangerous and have even been known to attack and kill humans. A Komodo uses its sense of smell to locate food, using its long, yellow tongue. A Komodo can consume 80 percent of its body weight in just one meal!

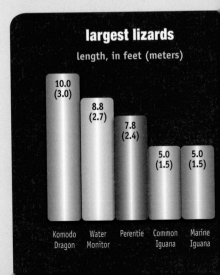

largest lizards

length, in feet (meters)

Komodo Dragon	Water Monitor	Perentie	Common Iguana	Marine Iguana
10.0 (3.0)	8.8 (2.7)	7.8 (2.4)	5.0 (1.5)	5.0 (1.5)

largest reptile

Saltwater Crocodile

Saltwater crocodiles can grow to 22 feet (6.7 m) long. That's about twice the length of the average car. However, males usually measure only about 17 feet (5 m) long, and females normally reach about 10 feet (3 m) in length. A large adult will feed on buffalo, monkeys, cattle, wild boar, and other large mammals. Saltwater crocodiles are found throughout the East Indies and Australia. Despite their name, saltwater crocodiles can also be found in fresh water and swamps. Some other common names for this species are the estuarine crocodile and the Indo-Pacific crocodile.

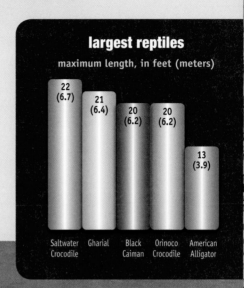

largest reptiles

maximum length, in feet (meters)

Saltwater Crocodile	Gharial	Black Caiman	Orinoco Crocodile	American Alligator
22 (6.7)	21 (6.4)	20 (6.2)	20 (6.2)	13 (3.9)

animals

largest spider

Goliath Birdeater

A Goliath birdeater is about the same size as a dinner plate—it can grow to a total length of 11 inches (28 cm) and weigh about 6 ounces (170 g). A Goliath's spiderlings are also big—they can have a 6-inch (15 cm) leg span just one year after hatching. These giant tarantulas are found mostly in the rain forests of Guyana, Suriname, Brazil, and Venezuela. The Goliath birdeater's name is misleading—they commonly eat insects and small reptiles. Similar to other tarantula species, the Goliath birdeater lives in a burrow. The spider will wait by the opening to ambush prey that gets too close.

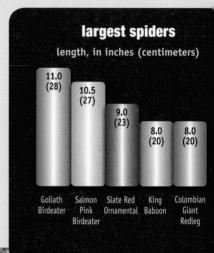

largest spiders

length, in inches (centimeters)

11.0 (28)	10.5 (27)	9.0 (23)	8.0 (20)	8.0 (20)
Goliath Birdeater	Salmon Pink Birdeater	Slate Red Ornamental	King Baboon	Colombian Giant Redleg

fastest-flying insect

Hawk Moth

The average hawk moth—which got its name from its swift and steady flight—can cruise along at speeds over 33 miles (53 km) per hour. That's faster than the average speed limit on most city streets. Although they are found throughout the world, most live in tropical climates. Also known as the sphinx moth and the hummingbird moth, this large insect can have a wingspan that reaches up to 8 inches (20 cm). The insect also has a good memory and may return to the same flowers at the same time each day.

fastest-flying insects

speed, in miles (kilometers) per hour

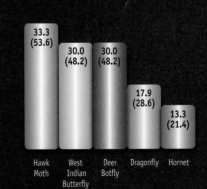

Hawk Moth	West Indian Butterfly	Deer Botfly	Dragonfly	Hornet
33.3 (53.6)	30.0 (48.2)	30.0 (48.2)	17.9 (28.6)	13.3 (21.4)

fastest-running insect

Australian Tiger Beetle

Australian tiger beetles can zip along at about 5.7 miles (9.2 km) per hour—that's about 170 body lengths per second! If a human could run at the same pace, he or she would run about 340 miles (547.2 km) per hour. Australian tiger beetles use their terrific speed to run down prey. Once a meal has been caught, the beetle chews it up in its powerful jaws and coats it in digestive juice. When the prey has become soft, the tiger beetle rolls it together and eats it. These fierce beetles, which got their name from their skillful hunting, will also bite humans when provoked.

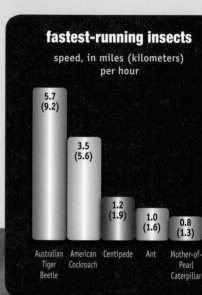

fastest-running insects

speed, in miles (kilometers) per hour

Australian Tiger Beetle	5.7 (9.2)
American Cockroach	3.5 (5.6)
Centipede	1.2 (1.9)
Ant	1.0 (1.6)
Mother-of-Pearl Caterpillar	0.8 (1.3)

longest insect migration

Monarch Butterfly

Millions of monarch butterflies travel to Mexico from all parts of North America every fall, flying as far as 2,700 miles (4,345 km). Once there, they will huddle together in the trees and wait out the cold weather. In spring and summer, most butterflies only live four or five weeks as adults, but in the fall, a special generation of monarchs is born. These butterflies will live for about seven months and participate in the great migration to Mexico. Scientists are studying these butterflies in the hope of learning how the insects know where and when to migrate to a place they have never visited before.

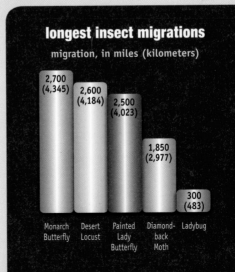

longest insect migrations

migration, in miles (kilometers)

2,700 (4,345)	2,600 (4,184)	2,500 (4,023)	1,850 (2,977)	300 (483)
Monarch Butterfly	Desert Locust	Painted Lady Butterfly	Diamond-back Moth	Ladybug

Dogs

There are 45.6 million households across the United States that own one or more dogs. That means that about 39 percent of homes in America have a pooch residing there. About 24 percent of these families own two dogs, while another 9 percent own three or more. When it comes to finding a dog, approximately 19 percent of families head to a shelter to adopt one. Those who prefer purebreds tend to choose Labrador retrievers, German shepherds, and Yorkshire terriers. Some of the most popular dog names include Max, Buddy, Rocky, and Bailey.

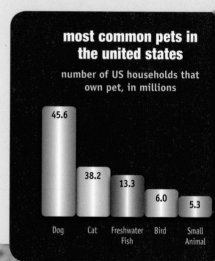

most common pets in the united states

number of US households that own pet, in millions

Dog	Cat	Freshwater Fish	Bird	Small Animal
45.6	38.2	13.3	6.0	5.3

most popular dog breed in the united states

Labrador Retriever

Labrador retrievers are top dog in the United States! In 2010, the American Kennel Club recorded more purebred dog registrations for labs than any other dog in the United States. Labs are very popular with families because of their gentle nature, and they are popular with hunters because of their retrieving skills. A very intelligent breed, Labrador retrievers can be trained to work in law enforcement or as guide dogs. They come in three colors— yellow, black, and brown—and are medium-size athletic dogs. They are considered by the American Kennel Club to be part of the sporting class.

most popular dog breeds in the united states

american kennel club rank

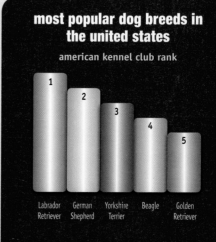

1	2	3	4	5
Labrador Retriever	German Shepherd	Yorkshire Terrier	Beagle	Golden Retriever

*most popular cat breed
in the united states*

Persian

The Cat Fanciers' Association—the world's largest registry of pedigree cats—ranks the Persian as the most popular cat in the country. These flat-faced cats are known for their gentle personalities, which make them popular family pets. Persians come in many colors, including silver, golden, smoke, and tabby. They have long hair, which requires continuous grooming and maintenance. These pets, like most other cat breeds, can live as long as 15 years.

most popular cat breeds in the united states

cat fanciers' association rank

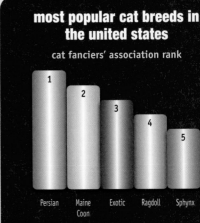

Persian	Maine Coon	Exotic	Ragdoll	Sphynx
1	2	3	4	5

Mount Rainier

Mount Rainier had a record snowfall of 1,224 inches (3,109 cm) between February 1971 and February 1972. That's enough snow to cover a ten-story building! Located in the Cascade Mountains of Washington State, Mount Rainier is actually a volcano buried under 35 square miles (90.7 sq km) of snow and ice. The mountain, which covers about 100 square miles (259 sq km), reaches a height of 14,410 feet (4,392 m). Its three peaks include Liberty Cap, Point Success, and Columbia Crest. Mount Rainier National Park was established in 1899.

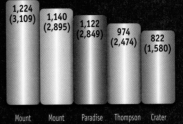

united states' greatest annual snowfalls

greatest annual snowfall, in inches (centimeters)

Mount Rainier, Washington, Feb. 1971–Feb. 1972	Mount Baker, Washington, 1998–1999	Paradise Station, Washington, July 1, 1971– June 30, 1972	Thompson Pass, Alaska, 1952–1953	Crater Lake National Park, Oregon 1948–1949
1,224 (3,109)	1,140 (2,895)	1,122 (2,849)	974 (2,474)	822 (1,580)

weather

coldest inhabited place

Resolute

The residents of Resolute, Canada, have to bundle up—the average temperature is just -11.6°F (-24.2°C). Located on the northeast shore of Resolute Bay on the south coast of Cornwallis Island, the community is commonly the starting point for expeditions to the North Pole. In the winter it can stay dark for 24 hours, and in the summer it can stay light during the entire night. Only about 200 people brave the climate year-round, but the area is becoming quite popular with tourists.

coldest inhabited places

average temperature, in degrees fahrenheit (celsius)

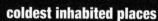

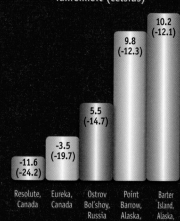

Resolute, Canada	Eureka, Canada	Ostrov Bol'shoy, Russia	Point Barrow, Alaska, USA	Barter Island, Alaska, USA
-11.6 (-24.2)	-3.5 (-19.7)	5.5 (-14.7)	9.8 (-12.3)	10.2 (-12.1)

hottest inhabited place

Dallol

Throughout the year, temperatures in Dallol, Ethiopia, average 93.2°F (34°C). Dallol is at the northernmost tip of the Great Rift Valley. The Dallol Depression reaches 328 feet (100 m) below sea level, making it the lowest point below sea level that is not covered by water. The area also has several active volcanoes. The only people to inhabit the region are the Afar, who have adapted to the harsh conditions there. For instance, to collect water, the women build covered stone piles and wait for condensation to form on the rocks.

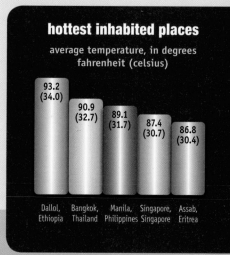

hottest inhabited places

average temperature, in degrees fahrenheit (celsius)

Dallol, Ethiopia	Bangkok, Thailand	Manila, Philippines	Singapore, Singapore	Assab, Eritrea
93.2 (34.0)	90.9 (32.7)	89.1 (31.7)	87.4 (30.7)	86.8 (30.4)

weather

wettest inhabited place

Lloro

Umbrellas are in constant use in Lloro, Colombia, where the average annual rainfall totals about 523 inches (1,328 cm). That's about 1.4 inches (3.5 cm) a day, totaling more than 43 feet (13 m) a year! Located in the northwestern part of the country, Lloro is near the Pacific Ocean and the Caribbean Sea. Trade winds help bring lots of moisture from the coasts to this tropical little town, creating the humidity and precipitation that soak this lowland. Lloro is home to about 7,000 people.

wettest inhabited places

average annual rainfall, in inches (centimeters)

523 (1,328)	498 (1,265)	467 (1,187)	460 (1,168)	405 (1,029)
Lloro, Colombia	Cherrapunji, India	Mawsynram, India	Waialeale, Hawaii, USA	Debundscha, Cameroon

driest inhabited place

Aswan

Each year, only 0.02 inches (0.5 mm) of rain falls on Aswan, Egypt. In the country's sunniest and southernmost city, summer temperatures can reach a blistering 114°F (46°C). Aswan is located on the west bank of the Nile River, and it has a very busy marketplace that is also popular with tourists. The Aswan High Dam, at 12,565 feet (3,830 m) long, is the city's most famous landmark. It produces the majority of Egypt's power in the form of hydroelectricity.

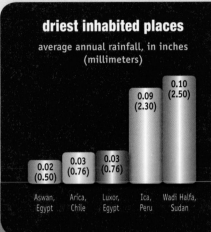

driest inhabited places

average annual rainfall, in inches (millimeters)

Aswan, Egypt	Arica, Chile	Luxor, Egypt	Ica, Peru	Wadi Halfa, Sudan
0.02 (0.50)	0.03 (0.76)	0.03 (0.76)	0.09 (2.30)	0.10 (2.50)

weather

place with the fastest winds

Barrow Island

On April 12, 1996, Cyclone Olivia blew through Barrow Island in Australia and created a wind gust that reached 253 miles (407 km) an hour. Barrow Island is about 30 miles (48 km) off the coast of Western Australia and is home to many endangered species, such as dugongs and green turtles. The dry, sandy land measures about 78 square miles (202 sq km) and is the second-largest island in Western Australia. Barrow Island also has hundreds of oil wells and is a top source of oil for the country. The island has produced more than 300 million barrels of oil since 1967.

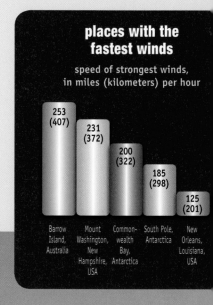

places with the fastest winds

speed of strongest winds, in miles (kilometers) per hour

Barrow Island, Australia	Mount Washington, New Hampshire, USA	Common-wealth Bay, Antarctica	South Pole, Antarctica	New Orleans, Louisiana, USA
253 (407)	231 (372)	200 (322)	185 (298)	125 (201)

tallest cactus

Saguaro

Many saguaro cacti grow to a height of 50 feet (15 m), but some have actually reached 75 feet (23 m). That's taller than a seven-story building. Saguaros start out quite small and grow very slowly. A saguaro reaches only about 1 inch (2.5 cm) high during its first 10 years. It will not bloom until it is between 50 and 75 years old. By this time, the cactus has a strong root system that can support about 9–10 tons (8–9 t) of growth. Its spines can measure up to 2.5 inches (5 cm) long. Saguaro cacti live for about 170 years. The giant cacti can be found from southeastern California to southern Arizona.

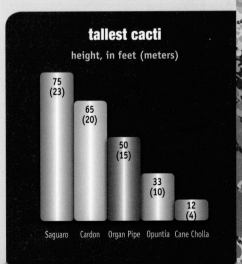

tallest cacti

height, in feet (meters)

Saguaro	Cardon	Organ Pipe	Opuntia	Cane Cholla
75 (23)	65 (20)	50 (15)	33 (10)	12 (4)

tallest tree

California Redwood

Growing in both California and southern Oregon, California redwoods can reach a height of 385 feet (117 m). Their trunks can grow up to 25 feet (8 m) in diameter. The tallest redwood on record is more than 60 feet (18 m) taller than the Statue of Liberty. Amazingly, this giant tree grows from a seed the size of a tomato. Some redwoods are believed to be more than 2,000 years old. The trees' thick bark and foliage protect them from natural hazards such as insects and fires.

tallest trees

height, in feet (meters)

California Redwood	Giant Sequoia	Eucalyptus	Douglas Fir	Japanese Cedar
385 (117)	350 (107)	300 (91)	250 (76)	175 (53)

most poisonous mushroom

Death Cap

Death cap mushrooms are members of the Amanita family, which are among the most dangerous mushrooms in the world. The death cap contains deadly peptide toxins that cause rapid loss of bodily fluids and intense thirst. Within six hours, the poison shuts down the kidneys, liver, and central nervous system, causing coma and—in more than 50 percent of cases—death. Estimates of the number of poisonous mushroom species range from 80 to 2,000. Most experts agree, however, that at least 100 varieties will cause severe symptoms and even death if eaten.

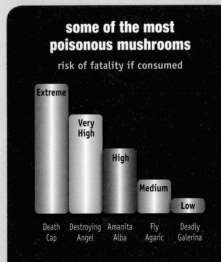

some of the most poisonous mushrooms

risk of fatality if consumed

Extreme	Very High	High	Medium	Low
Death Cap	Destroying Angel	Amanita Alba	Fly Agaric	Deadly Galerina

largest flower

Rafflesia

The blossoms of the giant rafflesia—or stinking corpse lily—can reach 36 inches (91 cm) in diameter and weigh up to 25 pounds (11 kg). Its petals can grow 1.5 feet (0.5 m) long and 1 inch (2.5 cm) thick. There are 16 different species of rafflesia. This endangered plant is found only in the rain forests of Borneo and Sumatra. It lives inside the bark of host vines and is noticeable only when its flowers break through to blossom. The large, reddish purple flowers give off a smell similar to rotting meat, which attracts insects that help spread the rafflesia's pollen.

largest flowers

size, in inches (centimeters)

Rafflesia	Sunflower	Giant Water Lily	Brazilian Dutchman	Magnolia
36 (91)	19 (48)	18 (46)	14 (36)	10 (25)

deadliest plant

Castor Bean

The castor bean plant produces seeds that contain a protein called ricin. Scientists estimate that ricin is about 6,000 times more poisonous than cyanide and 12,000 times more poisonous than rattlesnake venom. It would take a particle of ricin only about the size of a grain of sand to kill a 160-pound (73 kg) adult. The deadly beans are actually quite pretty and are sometimes used in jewelry. Castor bean plants grow in warmer climates and can reach a height of about 10 feet (3 m). Their leaves can measure up to 2 feet (0.6 m) wide.

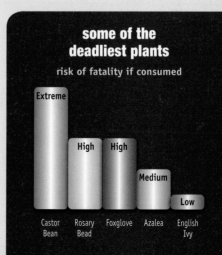

some of the deadliest plants

risk of fatality if consumed

Castor Bean	Rosary Bead	Foxglove	Azalea	English Ivy
Extreme	High	High	Medium	Low

plants

largest seed

Coco de Mer

Measuring 3 feet (1 m) in diameter and 12 inches (30 cm) in length, the giant, dark brown seed of the coco de mer palm tree can weigh up to 40 pounds (18 kg). Only a few thousand seeds are produced each year. Coco de mer trees are found on the island of Praslin in the Seychelles Archipelago of the Indian Ocean. The area where some of the few remaining trees grow has been declared a Natural World Heritage Site in an effort to protect the species from poachers looking for the rare seeds. The tree can grow up to 100 feet (31 m) tall, with leaves measuring 20 feet (6 m) long and 12 feet (3.6 m) wide.

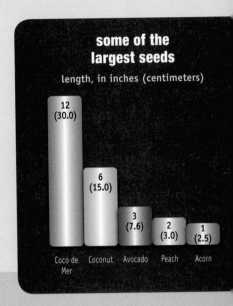

some of the largest seeds

length, in inches (centimeters)

Coco de Mer	Coconut	Avocado	Peach	Acorn
12 (30.0)	6 (15.0)	3 (7.6)	2 (3.0)	1 (2.5)

highest tsunami wave since 1900

Lituya Bay

A 1,720-foot (524 m) tsunami wave crashed down in Lituya Bay, Alaska, on July 9, 1958. Located in Glacier Bay National Park, the tsunami was caused by a massive landslide that was triggered by an 8.3-magnitude earthquake. The water from the bay covered 5 square miles (13 sq km) of land and traveled inland as far as 3,600 feet (1,097 m). Millions of trees were washed away. Amazingly, because the area was very isolated and the coastline was sheltered by coves, only two people died when their fishing boat sank.

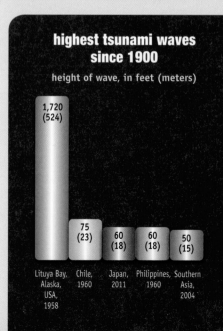

highest tsunami waves since 1900

height of wave, in feet (meters)

Lituya Bay, Alaska, USA, 1958	Chile, 1960	Japan, 2011	Philippines, 1960	Southern Asia, 2004
1,720 (524)	75 (23)	60 (18)	60 (18)	50 (15)

most intense earthquake since 1900

Chile

An explosive earthquake measuring 9.5 on the Richter scale rocked the coast of Chile on May 22, 1960. This is equal to the intensity of about 60,000 hydrogen bombs. Some 2,000 people were killed and another 3,000 injured. The death toll was fairly low because the foreshocks frightened people into the streets. When the massive jolt came, many of the buildings that collapsed were already empty. The coastal towns of Valdivia and Puerto Montt suffered the most damage because they were closest to the epicenter— located about 100 miles (161 km) offshore. On February 27, 2010, Chile was rocked by another huge earthquake (8.8 magnitude), but the loss of life and property was much less than from previous quakes.

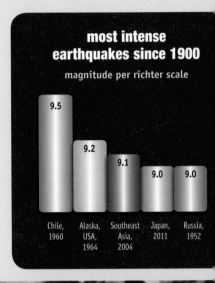

most intense earthquakes since 1900

magnitude per richter scale

Chile, 1960	Alaska, USA, 1964	Southeast Asia, 2004	Japan, 2011	Russia, 1952
9.5	9.2	9.1	9.0	9.0

most destructive flood since 1900

Hurricane Katrina

The pounding rain and storm surges of Hurricane Katrina resulted in catastrophic flooding that cost about $60 billion. The storm formed in late August 2005 over the Bahamas, moved across Florida, and finally hit Louisiana on August 29 as a category-three storm. The storm surge from the Gulf of Mexico flooded the state, as well as neighboring Alabama and Mississippi. Many levees could not hold back the massive amounts of water, and entire towns were destroyed. In total, some 1,800 people lost their lives.

most destructive floods since 1900

cost of damages, in billions of US dollars

60	30	27	24	18
Hurricane Katrina, USA, 2005	Yangtze River, China, 1998	Bangladesh, 1970	Yangtze River, China, 1990	Great Midwest Flood, USA, 1993

disasters

worst oil spill

Gulf War

During the Gulf War in 1991, Iraqi troops opened valves of oil wells in Kuwait, releasing more than 240 million gallons (908 million L) of oil into the Persian Gulf. At its worst, the spill measured 101 miles by 42 miles (163 km by 68 km) and was about 5 inches (13 cm) thick. Some of the oil eventually evaporated, another 1 million barrels were collected out of the water, and the rest washed ashore. Although much of the oil can no longer be seen, most of it remains, soaked into the deeper layers of sand along the coast. Amazingly, the wildlife that lives in these areas were not harmed as much as was initially feared. However, salt marsh areas without strong currents were hit the hardest, as oil collected there and killed off entire ecosystems.

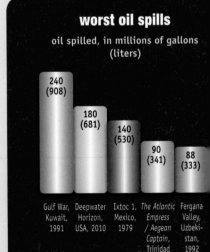

worst oil spills

oil spilled, in millions of gallons (liters)

240 (908)	180 (681)	140 (530)	90 (341)	88 (333)
Gulf War, Kuwait, 1991	Deepwater Horizon, USA, 2010	Ixtoc 1, Mexico, 1979	*The Atlantic Empress / Aegean Captain,* Trinidad & Tobago, 1979	Fergana Valley, Uzbekistan, 1992

Oklahoma City

On May 3, 1999, a devastating tornado swept through downtown Oklahoma City, Oklahoma, killing 36 people and causing more than $1.2 billion in damages. This powerful twister traveled almost 38 miles (61 km) in four hours and measured 1 mile (1.6 km) wide at times. With raging winds reaching 318 miles (512 km) per hour, it was the strongest wind speed ever recorded. More than 800 houses were destroyed in Oklahoma City alone. Because of the mass destruction caused by this twister, it was classified as a 5—the second-highest possible rating—on the Fujita Tornado Scale.

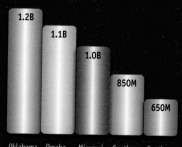

most destructive tornadoes since 1900

cost of damages, in US dollars

1.2B	1.1B	1.0B	850M	650M
Oklahoma City, Oklahoma, 1999	Omaha, Nebraska, 1975	Missouri, Illinois, Indiana, 1925	Southern USA, 2008	Southern USA, 2006

disasters

Devastation from
Hurricane Camille

most intense hurricanes since 1900

Hurricane Allen &
Hurricane Camille

Both Hurricane Allen and Hurricane
Camille were category 5 storms
with winds that gusted up to 190 miles
(306 km) per hour. Hurricane Camille
made landfall in the United States along
the mouth of the Mississippi River on
August 17, 1969. Mississippi and Virginia
sustained the most damage, and the
total storm damages cost $1.42 billion.
Hurricane Allen sustained its strongest
winds near Puerto Rico on August 5,
1980. The storm traveled through the
Caribbean, Cuba, the Yucatan Peninsula,
and the south-central United States.
The damages totaled about $1 billion.

most intense
hurricanes since 1900

highest sustained wind speeds,
in miles (kilometers) per hour

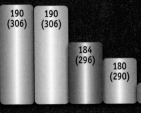

Hurricane Allen, 1980	Hurricane Camille, 1969	Hurricane Gilbert, 1988	Hurricane Mitch, 1998	Hurricane Katrina, 2005
190 (306)	190 (306)	184 (296)	180 (290)	175 (282)

Car Batteries

More than 95 percent of all used lead-acid car batteries in the United States are brought to recycling centers instead of being tossed in the trash. This is very good news for the environment because lead is a poisonous metal that can cause several illnesses if it seeps into soil or water that people use. About 97 percent of the lead found in a battery can be recycled. Other parts of the battery can be recycled as well, including sulfuric acid, which can be converted into sodium sulfate, used in fertilizers. Each year, Americans replace approximately 100 million car batteries.

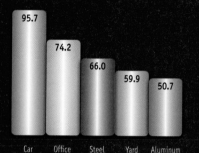

most recycled items in the united states

percentage of item recycled

Car Batteries	Office Paper	Steel Cans	Yard Trimmings	Aluminum Cans
95.7	74.2	66.0	59.9	50.7

money records

most expensive • most valuable • big business

most expensive hotel

Royal Penthouse Suite

Guests better bring their wallets to the President Wilson Hotel in Geneva, Switzerland—the Royal Penthouse Suite costs $65,000 a night! That means a weeklong stay would total $455,000, which is almost twice the price of buying the average house. The suite is reserved for heads of state and celebrities, and offers beautiful views of the Alps and Lake Geneva. The 18,082-square-foot (1,680 sq m) four-bedroom luxury suite has a private elevator and marble bathrooms. The state-of-the-art security system includes bulletproof doors and windows.

most expensive hotels

cost per night, in US dollars

65,000	50,000	40,000	40,000	35,000
Royal Penthouse Suite, President Wilson Hotel, Switzerland	Royal Villa, Grand Resort Lagonessi, Greece	Presidential Suite, Raj Palace, India	Hugh Hefner Sky Villa, Palms Casino & Resort, USA	Ty Warner Penthouse, Four Seasons, USA

most expensive cell phone

Stuart Hughes iPhone 4 Diamond Rose Edition

For the multimillionaire who has everything, the Stuart Hughes iPhone 4 Diamond Rose Edition can be purchased for about $8.1 million. At a price like that, the buyer better not misplace it! The edge of this dazzling phone is decorated with 500 tiny diamonds that total 100 carats, and its back is made of rose gold. The iconic Apple logo is formed from an additional 53 diamonds. Instead of a button, there is a 7.4-carat pink diamond that navigates the screen. Another 8-carat flawless diamond comes with the phone and can replace the pink one as the navigator. The phone comes in a pink granite box lined with brushed leather.

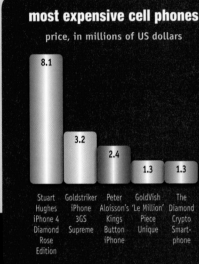

most expensive cell phones

price, in millions of US dollars

Stuart Hughes iPhone 4 Diamond Rose Edition	Goldstriker iPhone 3GS Supreme	Peter Aloisson's Kings Button iPhone	GoldVish 'Le Million' Piece Unique	The Diamond Crypto Smart-phone
8.1	3.2	2.4	1.3	1.3

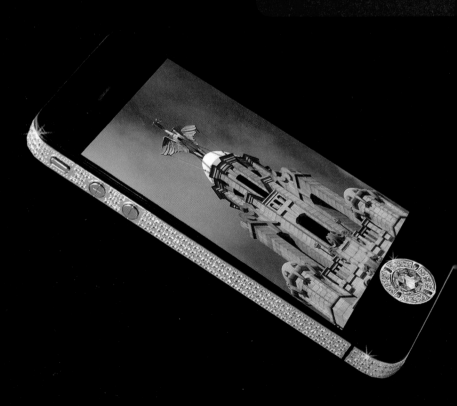

celebrity with the most expensive tweets

Eva Longoria

Desperate Housewives star Eva Longoria raised more than $32,000 for charity when she participated in Twitchange—a ten-day auction during October 2010 in which people could bid on one of 178 stars' Tweets. Fans bid on the chance to be followed, mentioned, or Retweeted by their favorite celebrities. The auction raised a total of $540,000 through 13,000 bids collected on eBay. The campaign received more than 35 million web hits in just four weeks. The funds benefit a nonprofit organization that is building a school for special-needs children in Haiti.

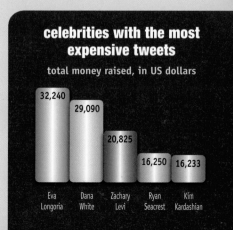

celebrities with the most expensive tweets

total money raised, in US dollars

Eva Longoria	Dana White	Zachary Levi	Ryan Seacrest	Kim Kardashian
32,240	29,090	20,825	16,250	16,233

most expensive bicycle

"Butterfly" Trek Madone

The "Butterfly" Trek Madone bike sold for $500,000 at a Sotheby's auction that raised money for the Lance Armstrong Foundation to fight cancer. The bike, ridden by Lance Armstrong in the final leg of the 2009 Tour de France, was designed by artist Damien Hurst. He used hundreds of real butterfly wings and pink LIVESTRONG logos to decorate the frame and rims of the bike. There was some controversy over the creation of this bike when PETA (People for the Ethical Treatment of Animals) raised concerns about real animals being used for decoration. A basic Trek Madone costs about $4,000.

most expensive bicycles

price, in US dollars

"Butter-fly" Trek Madone	Trek Yoshitomo Nara Speed Concept	Aurumania Crystal Edition Gold Bike	Trek Madone 7-Diamond	Montante Luxury Gold Collection
500,000	200,000	101,000	75,000	46,000

most expensive comic book

Action Comics, No. 1

Action Comics, No. 1 sold for $1.5 million at auction in March 2010. This comic was published in April 1938 and introduced Superman to the world. Known as the world's first superhero comic, it featured the Man of Steel lifting up a car on its cover. It originally sold for 10 cents. Comic artists Jerry Siegel and Joe Shuster created the book and were paid $10 per page. About 200,000 copies were printed, but only about 100 survive today. Another copy of the same issue was auctioned off in February 2010, but fetched only $1 million because it was not in good condition.

most expensive comic books

price, in US dollars

1.50M	1.38M	1.00M	671,000	430,000
Action Comics, No. 1	Detective Comics, No. 27	Action Comics, No. 1	Superman, No. 1	All-American Comics, No. 16

most expensive production car

Bugatti Veyron 16.4 Super Sport

The Bugatti Veyron Super Sport costs a cool $2.6 million. This basic model of this pricey machine debuted in 2005, and the Super Sport edition was introduced in 2010. The Veyron Super Sport has some impressive specifications, including 1,200 horsepower. The car also features a twin clutch gearbox with seven speeds, and the four enlarged superchargers boost the powerful 16-valve engine. Only 30 Veyron Super Sports will be produced as they are ordered. The first 5 will be orange and black, which is the same color scheme of the prototype used to introduce the model.

most expensive production cars

price, in millions of US dollars

Bugatti Veyron 16.4 Super Sport	Lamborghini Reventon	Koenigsegg Agera	Maybach Landaulet	Pagani Zonda C9
2.6	1.6	1.5	1.4	1.3

most expensive motorcycle

Ecosse Titanium Series RR Limited Edition

With a sticker price of $275,000, the Ecosse Titanium Series RR Limited Edition is the most expensive production motorcycle in history. This incredibly powerful bike boasts a carbon fiber–coated titanium chassis and a 2150cc engine with up to 200 horsepower. To complement the motorcycle, world-renown French watchmaker BRM developed a timepiece that matches the bike's design and coloring. Each of the ten bikes produced will have a specialized watch that corresponds to it, and the cycle's serial number will be inscribed on the back of the timepiece.

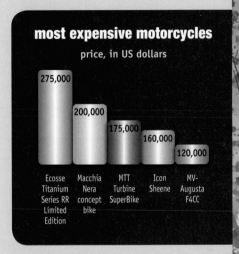

most expensive motorcycles

price, in US dollars

275,000	200,000	175,000	160,000	120,000
Ecosse Titanium Series RR Limited Edition	Macchia Nera concept bike	MTT Turbine SuperBike	Icon Sheene	MV-Augusta F4CC

most valuable sports franchise

Manchester United

English soccer team Manchester United Football Club is valued at $1.83 billion and brought in $459 million in revenue during the season. The club was founded in 1878, and it has since won 18 league titles and a record 11 FA (Football Association) Challenge Cups. Nicknamed the Red Devils, they were also the first English football club to win the European Cup when they were victorious in 1968. Manchester United is hugely popular with fans and boasts the highest average home attendance in Europe.

most valuable sports franchises

value, in billions of US dollars

Manchester United	Dallas Cowboys	New York Yankees	Wash-ington Redskins	New England Patriots
1.83	1.65	1.60	1.55	1.36

most valuable piece of sports memorabilia

Naismith's "Rules of Basketball"

Dr. James Naismith, a YMCA physical education teacher who invented the game of basketball in 1891, wrote out the basics of the game in a document entitled "Founding Rules of Basketball." In 2010, that two-page document sold for more than $4.3 million at auction. The document was purchased by billionaire David Booth, who plans to bring it to the University of Kansas, where Naismith coached basketball for about 20 years. Since the game was invented, many of Naismith's rules have been changed, including number of players, amount of physical contact, and the addition of dribbling.

most valuable sports memorabilia

price at auction, in US dollars

Memorabilia	Price
Naismith's "Rules of Basketball"	4.33M
Mark McGwire's 70th Home-Run Ball	3.00M
T206 Honus Wagner Tobacco Card	2.35M
Babe Ruth's 1st Home-Run Bat	1.26M
Babe Ruth's 1933 1st All-Star Game Home-Run Ball	805,000

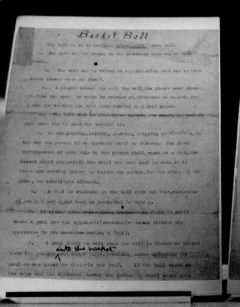

big business

Ford F-Series

Ford sold 528,349 F-Series trucks during 2010. The F-Series originated in 1948, when the F-1 (half ton), the F-2 (three-quarter ton), and the F-3 (Heavy Duty) were introduced. Since then, many modifications and new editions have been introduced, including the F-150. The modern F-150 sports a V-8 engine and the option of a regular, extended, or crew cab. The bed size ranges from 5.5 feet (1.6 m) to 8 feet (2.4 km). The Platinum F-150—the top-of-the-line version—features platinum chrome wheels, a fancy grille design, leather upholstery, and heated seats.

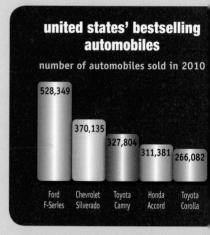

united states' bestselling automobiles

number of automobiles sold in 2010

528,349				
	370,135			
		327,804		
			311,381	266,082
Ford F-Series	Chevrolet Silverado	Toyota Camry	Honda Accord	Toyota Corolla

largest global retailer

Wal-Mart

Megadiscount retail chain Wal-Mart had more than $408 billion in sales during 2010. Wal-Mart serves more than 200 million customers each week at its more than 8,000 stores. Located in 15 countries, the company employs more than 1.4 million people in the United States and another 700,000 worldwide. This makes Wal-Mart one of the largest private employers in North America. Wal-Mart also believes in giving back to the community and donated more than $400 million to local charities in 2010. Wal-Mart is currently ranked number one in the Fortune 500 list of most profitable companies.

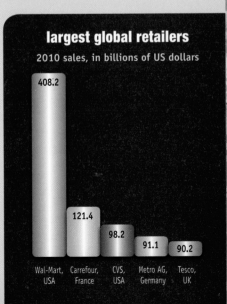

largest global retailers

2010 sales, in billions of US dollars

Wal-Mart, USA	Carrefour, France	CVS, USA	Metro AG, Germany	Tesco, UK
408.2	121.4	98.2	91.1	90.2

largest global food franchise

McDonald's

With its "golden arches" in 32,478 locations around the world, McDonald's is the largest global food franchise. In 2010, McDonald's enjoyed $24 billion in worldwide sales from its 13,980 domestic restaurants and 18,498 international restaurants. The first McDonald's restaurant was opened by Ray Kroc in April 1955 in Des Plaines, Illinois. Today, the fast food giant serves more than 60 million people in 117 countries each day. McDonald's employs about 1.7 million people worldwide, and more than three-quarters of all McDonald's are owned and operated by local residents.

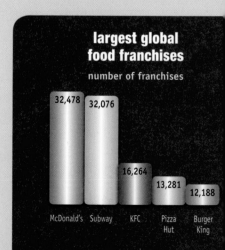

largest global food franchises

number of franchises

McDonald's	Subway	KFC	Pizza Hut	Burger King
32,478	32,076	16,264	13,281	12,188

largest retail franchise

7-Eleven

There are 37,357 7-Eleven convenience stores located around the world. Approximately 96 percent of these stores are franchised, with 5,900 locations in the United States and 31,457 locations internationally. 7-Eleven earned $58.9 billion in sales in 2010. The store chain is ranked number two on the Forbes Top Franchise for the Money list, meaning that investors have a very good chance of making a profit on their stores. The stores sell about 275 baked goods every minute, more than 2,300 fresh sandwiches each hour, and 13 million Slurpee beverages each month. Approximately 25 percent of Americans live within a mile (1.6 km) of a 7-Eleven store.

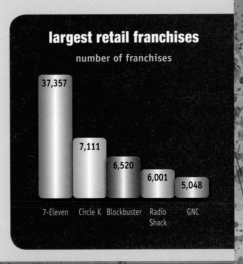

largest retail franchises
number of franchises

7-Eleven	Circle K	Blockbuster	Radio Shack	GNC
37,357	7,111	6,520	6,001	5,048

human-made records

structures • travel • transportation • cities

amusement park with the most rides

Cedar Point

Located in Sandusky, Ohio, Cedar Point offers park visitors 75 rides to enjoy. Windseeker—the park's newest ride—is a 300-foot (91 m) swing above Cedar Point Beach. Top Thrill Dragster roller coaster is the second tallest in the world at 420 feet (128 m). And with 17 roller coasters, Cedar Point also has the most coasters of any theme park in the world. Over 53,963 feet (16,448 m) of coaster track—more than 10 miles (16.1 km)—run through the park. In 2008, Cedar Point was named Best Amusement Park in the World by *Amusement Today* for the 11th time.

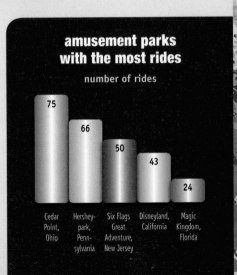

amusement parks with the most rides

number of rides

Cedar Point, Ohio	Hershey-park, Penn-sylvania	Six Flags Great Adventure, New Jersey	Disneyland, California	Magic Kingdom, Florida
75	66	50	43	24

city with the most skyscrapers

Hong Kong

A total of 207 skyscrapers rises high above the streets of Hong Kong. In fact, the world's fifth-tallest building—Two International Finance Centre—towers 1,362 feet (415 m) above the city. Because this bustling Chinese business center has only about 160 square miles (414 sq km) of land suitable for building, architects have to build up instead of out. And Hong Kong keeps growing—65 of the city's giant buildings were constructed in the last eight years. Some large development projects, such as the Sky Tower Apartment Complex, added seven skyscrapers to the landscape in just one year.

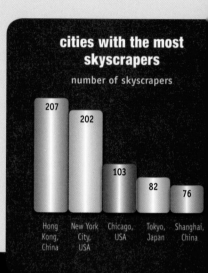

cities with the most skyscrapers

number of skyscrapers

City	Number
Hong Kong, China	207
New York City, USA	202
Chicago, USA	103
Tokyo, Japan	82
Shanghai, China	76

Q1 (on right)

tallest apartment building

Q1

Q1, a luxury apartment complex on Australia's Gold Coast, rises 1,058 feet (323 m) above the surrounding sand. There are 526 apartments within the building's 80 floors. Some apartments have glass-enclosed balconies. Q1 residents can enjoy Australia's only beachside observation deck and a ten-story sky garden. Some other amenities include retail outlets, a lagoon swimming pool, a spa, a sauna, and a fitness center. And just in case all nine elevators are out of order, there are 1,430 steps from the penthouse to the basement!

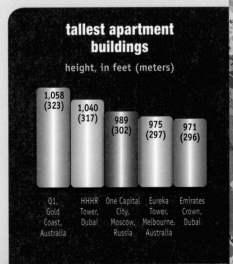

tallest apartment buildings

height, in feet (meters)

1,058 (323)	1,040 (317)	989 (302)	975 (297)	971 (296)
Q1, Gold Coast, Australia	HHHR Tower, Dubai	One Capital City, Moscow, Russia	Eureka Tower, Melbourne, Australia	Emirates Crown, Dubai

structures

largest dome

02

Located in London, UK, the 02 has a roof that measures 1,050 feet (320 m) in diameter and covers 861,113 square feet (80,000 sq m). That's large enough to contain the Great Pyramid of Giza! The roof is made of 107,639 square feet (10,000 sq m) of fabric and is held up by 43 miles of steel cable. The dome is currently being used as a concert venue, hosting such acts as Bon Jovi, Rihanna, and Aerosmith. It also boasts a movie complex, theaters, and restaurants. The dome was built for the country's millennium celebration. After the New Year's celebration, renovations began to turn the dome into a sports complex, and it will be used for the 2012 Olympics.

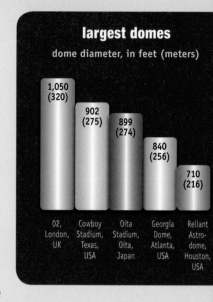

largest domes
dome diameter, in feet (meters)

1,050 (320)	902 (275)	899 (274)	840 (256)	710 (216)
02, London, UK	Cowboy Stadium, Texas, USA	Oita Stadium, Oita, Japan	Georgia Dome, Atlanta, USA	Reliant Astro-dome, Houston, USA

tallest hotel

Rose Tower

The Rose Tower—which is also known as Rose Rayhaan by Rotana—rises 1,093 feet (333 meters) above the bustling streets and desert that surround it. The world's tallest hotel was built in 2007, but officially opened in 2009. It is located in Dubai, United Arab Emirates, and is Rayhaan's flagship hotel. It features 72 floors that house 482 rooms and suites. There are three restaurants for guests to enjoy, in addition to a swimming pool, a fitness club, and conference facilities. The postmodern skyscraper has a glass exterior, and includes a nine-level parking garage. It cost more than $180 million to build this architectural wonder.

tallest hotels
height, in feet (meters)

Rose Tower, Dubai, UAE	1,093 (333)
Ryugyong Hotel, Pyongyang, North Korea	1,083 (330)
Burj Al Arab, Dubai, UAE	1,053 (321)
Jumeirah Emirates Towers, Dubai, UAE	1,014 (309)
Baiyoke Tower II, Bangkok, Thailand	997 (304)

tallest habitable building

Burj Khalifa

The recently constructed Burj Khalifa in the United Arab Emirates towers 2,684 feet (818 m) above the ground. With 110 floors, the building cost about $4.1 billion to construct. Both a hotel and apartments are housed inside the luxury building, which covers 500 acres (202 ha). The building features the world's fastest elevators, traveling at a speed of 40 miles (64 km) an hour. The tower supplies its occupants with about 250,000 gallons (66,043 L) of water a day, and delivers enough electricity to power 360,000 100-watt lightbulbs.

tallest habitable buildings

height, in feet (meters)

2,684 (818)	1,666 (508)	1,614 (492)	1,588 (484)	1,483 (452)
Burj Khalifa, UAE	Taipei 101, Taiwan	Shanghai World Financial Center, China	International Commerce Centre, Hong Kong	Petronas Twin Towers, Malaysia

largest swimming pool

San Alfonso Del Mar

The gigantic swimming pool at the San Alfonso del Mar resort, in Chile, spreads over 19.7 acres (8 ha). The monstrous pool is the equivalent to 6,000 standard swimming pools and holds 66 million gallons (250 million L) of water. In addition to swimming, guests can sail and scuba dive in the saltwater lagoon, which is surrounded by white sand beaches. And no diving for pennies here—the deep end measures 115 feet (35 m). The pool took five years to complete and first opened in December 2006. The project cost $2 billion to complete, and costs about $4 million annually to maintain it.

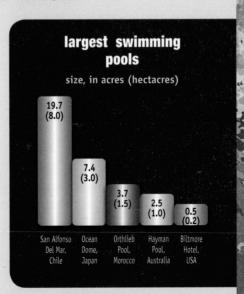

largest swimming pools

size, in acres (hectacres)

San Alfonso Del Mar, Chile	Ocean Dome, Japan	Orthlieb Pool, Morocco	Hayman Pool, Australia	Biltmore Hotel, USA
19.7 (8.0)	7.4 (3.0)	3.7 (1.5)	2.5 (1.0)	0.5 (0.2)

largest sports stadium

Rungrado May First Stadium

The Rungrado May First Stadium, also known as the May Day Stadium, can seat up to 150,000 people. The interior of the stadium covers 2.2 million square feet (204,386 sq m). Located in Pyongyang, North Korea, this venue is mostly used for soccer matches and other athletic contests. It is named after Rungra Island, on which the stadium is located, in the middle of the Taedong River. When it is not being used for sporting events, the stadium is used for a two-month festival known as Arirang.

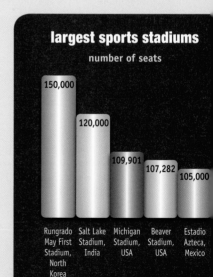

largest sports stadiums

number of seats

150,000	120,000	109,901	107,282	105,000
Rungrado May First Stadium, North Korea	Salt Lake Stadium, India	Michigan Stadium, USA	Beaver Stadium, USA	Estadio Azteca, Mexico

largest movie theater

Radio City Music Hall

New York City's Radio City Music Hall is the largest single-screen theater in the world, with 5,933 seats. It's no wonder that the theater has become a hot spot for films. Since 1933, more than 700 movies have opened there, including *Mary Poppins*, *101 Dalmatians*, and *The Lion King*. The massive theater has a marquee that measures a full city block in length, and its auditorium is 160 feet (49 m) long. Its ceilings tower 84 feet (26 m) high. Since it first opened, more than 300 million people have attended shows and films there.

largest movie theaters

number of seats

Radio City Music Hall, New York City, USA	Fox Theatre, Detroit, USA	Fox Theatre, St. Louis, USA	Cine Teatro Gran Rex, Buenos Aires, Argentina	Opera House, Boston, USA
5,933	5,045	4,500	3,350	2,907

most-visited amusement park

Magic Kingdom

Walt Disney World's Magic Kingdom in Orlando, Florida, entertains more than 17 million visitors annually. The park is made up of six areas, including Tomorrowland, Adventureland, Fantasyland, Frontierland, Liberty Square, and Main Street USA. Magic Kingdom offers a mix of thrill rides—such as Space Mountain, Splash Mountain, and Big Thunder Mountain Railroad—as well as family fun rides—such as "it's a small world," Dumbo the Flying Elephant, and Peter Pan's Flight. In addition, there are several restaurants and places to meet the famous Disney characters. The park opened in 1971 and covers about 107 acres (43 ha).

most-visited amusement parks

annual attendance, in millions

Magic Kingdom, USA	Disneyland, USA	Tokyo Disneyland, Japan	Disneyland Paris, France	Tokyo DisneySea, Japan
17.23	15.90	13.60	12.70	12.00

top tourist country

France

France hosts almost 79 million tourists annually. That's about two and a half times the entire population of Canada! The most popular French destinations are Paris and the Mediterranean coast. In July and August—the most popular months to visit France—tourists flock to the westernmost coastal areas of the region. In the winter, visitors hit the slopes at major ski resorts in the northern Alps. Tourists also visit many of France's world-renowned landmarks and monuments, including the Eiffel Tower, Notre Dame, the Louvre, and the Palace of Versailles. Most tourists are from other European countries, especially Germany.

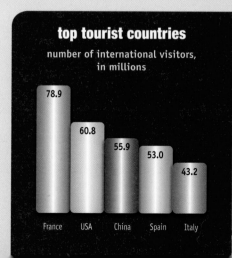

top tourist countries

number of international visitors, in millions

France	78.9
USA	60.8
China	55.9
Spain	53.0
Italy	43.2

united states' most-visited city

Orlando

About 48 million tourists vacation in sunny Orlando, Florida, annually. Orlando has countless attractions that appeal to all age groups, but some of the most popular include Disney World (47 million visitors), Sea World (6 million visitors), and Universal Studios (10 million visitors). Visitors spend about $27.6 billion each year, and tourism creates about 380,000 jobs in Orlando. The city has about 450 hotels and resorts that have a combined total of 114,000 rooms. About 38 million people fly into Orlando International Airport each year.

united states' most-visited cities

number of annual visitors, in millions

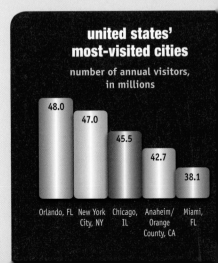

Orlando, FL	New York City, NY	Chicago, IL	Anaheim/ Orange County, CA	Miami, FL
48.0	47.0	45.5	42.7	38.1

travel

Great Smoky Mountains National Park

Almost 9.5 million visitors enjoyed the beauty of Great Smoky Mountains National Park during 2010. Spread between Tennessee and North Carolina, the park covers more than 521,085 acres (210,875 ha) and features 16 mountain peaks with elevations above 6,000 feet (1,829 m). There are more than 800 miles (1,287 km) of hiking trails throughout the park, which give visitors a chance to glimpse some of the bears, deer, elks, and other wildlife that live in the Great Smoky Mountains. More than 240 species of birds have been found in the park, and 60 of them live there year-round.

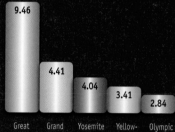

united states' most-visited national parks

number of annual visitors, in millions

9.46				
Great Smoky Mountains, Tennessee– North Carolina	Grand Canyon National Park, Arizona	Yosemite National Park, California	Yellow- stone National Park, Wyoming– Montana– Idaho	Olympic National Park, Washing- ton
	4.41	4.04	3.41	2.84

country with the most airports

United States

There are 15,079 airports located in the United States. That is more than the number of airports for the other nine top countries combined. The top two busiest airports in the world are also located in the United States. Altogether, US airports serve more than 709 million domestic travelers a year. With the threat of terrorism and the state of the economy, the airline industry lost $10 billion in 2002. In September 2005, rising fuel costs and competition from discount airlines caused several major airlines to file for bankruptcy. Since that time, the airline industry has seen limited growth and profits, mainly due to the country's sluggish economy.

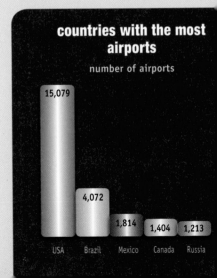

countries with the most airports

number of airports

Country	Number of airports
USA	15,079
Brazil	4,072
Mexico	1,814
Canada	1,404
Russia	1,213

Hartsfield-Jackson Atlanta International Airport

The Hartsfield-Jackson Atlanta International Airport serves about 88 million travelers in one year. That's more people than are living in California, Texas, and Florida combined. Approximately 967,050 planes depart and arrive at this airport every year. With parking lots, runways, maintenance facilities, and other buildings, the Hartsfield terminal complex covers about 130 acres (53 ha). Hartsfield-Jackson Atlanta International Airport has a north and a south terminal, an underground train, and six concourses with a total of 154 domestic and 28 international gates.

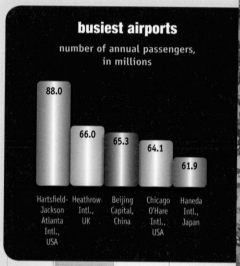

busiest airports

number of annual passengers, in millions

Airport	Passengers
Hartsfield-Jackson Atlanta Intl., USA	88.0
Heathrow Intl., UK	66.0
Beijing Capital, China	65.3
Chicago O'Hare Intl., USA	64.1
Haneda Intl., Japan	61.9

busiest airline

Delta

Delta Air Lines flew more than 162 million passengers to their destinations in 2010. With approximately 5,600 flights each day, Delta travels to more than 357 destinations in 66 countries. The company operates about 728 aircraft and employs more than 80,000 people. Delta's headquarters and largest hub is located in Atlanta, Georgia, but it has nine additional hubs worldwide. Forbes recently ranked Delta first in their annual World's Most Admired Airline Companies list. Delta's annual revenue in 2010 totaled $31.8 billion.

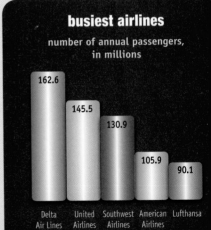

busiest airlines
number of annual passengers, in millions

Delta Air Lines	United Airlines	Southwest Airlines	American Airlines	Lufthansa
162.6	145.5	130.9	105.9	90.1

China

China leads the world in car production by creating 13.7 million vehicles annually. Approximately 44 percent of all the cars produced in the country are Chinese brands, including Lifan, Geely, Chery, and several others. International brands with factories in China include Volkswagen, General Motors, and Honda. Most of the cars that are produced in China are also sold there. Fewer than 400,000 cars are exported each year. China's growth in the car production industry is fairly recent. Since the country joined the World Trade Organization in 2001, China's car production has grown by about 1 million vehicles annually.

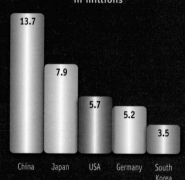

countries that produce the most cars

number of cars produced annually, in millions

China	Japan	USA	Germany	South Korea
13.7	7.9	5.7	5.2	3.5

transportation

Times Sq-42 St Station
S N Q R W
1 2 3 7
♿Elevator to N Q R W at 42 St
For A C E enter at 8 Avenue

Enter with or buy MetroCard
6am-12 midnight or see
agent at 42 St & 7 Av

city with the longest subway system

New York City

The New York subway system consists of
660 miles (1,062.2 km) of track—more
than enough to run from the Big Apple to
Louisville, Kentucky. An additional 182 miles
(292.9 km) of track lie beneath the city
streets, but they are not currently in use. New
York City has 468 subway stations, which is
just 35 fewer than the number of all other US
stations combined. There are approximately
6,380 subway cars in use, and together they
travel about 344.5 million miles (569.2
million km) annually. The New York City
subway system opened in 1904 with 9 miles
(14.5 km) of track and charged just
five cents per ride.

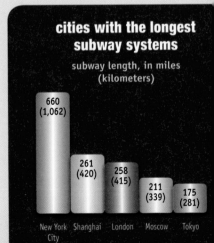

cities with the longest subway systems

subway length, in miles (kilometers)

City	Length
New York City	660 (1,062)
Shanghai	261 (420)
London	258 (415)
Moscow	211 (339)
Tokyo	175 (281)

Tokyo

Every year, more than 3 billion riders pack into the Tokyo subway. The system operates more than 2,500 cars and 282 subway stations. The tracks run for 175 miles (281 km). The Tokyo underground railroad opened in 1927. It has expanded through the years to include nine subway lines that connect the bustling areas of Chiyoda, Minato, and Chuo. The Tokyo Metro has recently taken steps to upgrade its cars and stations, reinforcing car frames and redesigning station platforms.

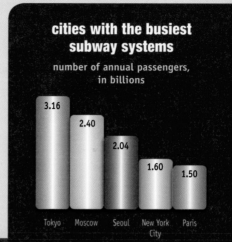

cities with the busiest subway systems

number of annual passengers, in billions

Tokyo	Moscow	Seoul	New York City	Paris
3.16	2.40	2.04	1.60	1.50

transportation

greenest city

Reykjavík

The Icelandic city of Reykjavík was ranked the greenest city in the world by *GlobalPost* because of its commitment to reducing its carbon footprint and its pledge to improve the environment. Reykjavík runs almost entirely on geothermal power and hydroelectricity. In its quest to become the most environmentally responsible city in Europe, Reykjavík uses only hydrogen-powered buses. The university has also begun integrating environmental issues and sustainability into most classes. The city is made up of about 170,000 people, which is about 60 percent of the country's population.

greenest cities

as ranked by *globalpost*

Reykjavík, Iceland	Portland, USA	Curitiba, Brazil	Malmo, Sweden	Van-couver, Canada
1	2	3	4	5

US
records

alabama to wyoming

state with the oldest mardi gras celebration

Alabama

People in Mobile, Alabama, have been celebrating Mardi Gras since 1703, although they did not have an official parade event until 1831. After a brief hiatus during the Civil War, the celebrations started back up in 1866 and have been growing ever since. Today, some 100,000 people gather in Mobile to enjoy the 40 parades that take place during the two weeks that lead up to Mardi Gras. On the biggest day—Fat Tuesday—six parades wind through the downtown waterfront, with floats and costumed dancers. But at the stroke of midnight, the partying stops and plans for the next year begin.

united states' oldest mardi gras celebrations

number of years since celebration bega

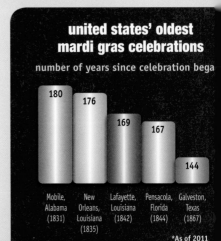

Mobile, Alabama (1831)	New Orleans, Louisiana (1835)	Lafayette, Louisiana (1842)	Pensacola, Florida (1844)	Galveston, Texas (1867)
180	176	169	167	144

*As of 2011

Alaska

The Tongass National Forest covers approximately 16,800,000 acres (6,798,900 ha) in southeast Alaska. That's about the same size as West Virginia. It is also home to the world's largest temperate rain forest. Some of the forest's trees are more than 700 years old. About 11,000 miles (17,703 km) of shoreline are inside the park. Some of the animals that live in the forest include bears, salmon, and wolves. The world's largest concentration of bald eagles also spend the fall and winter here on the Chilkat River.

US records

united states' largest national forests

size, in millions of acres (hectares)

Forest	Size
Tongass National Forest, Alaska	16.8 (6.8)
Humboldt-Toiyabe National Forest, California/Nevada	6.3 (1.5)
Chugach National Forest, Alaska	5.5 (2.2)
Tonto National Forest, Arizona	2.8 (1.1)
Boise National Forest, Idaho	2.6 (1.1)

state with the largest collection of telescopes

Arizona

The Kitt Peak National Observatory is home to 21 different telescopes—19 optical telescopes and 2 radio telescopes. Located above the Sonora Desert, the site was chosen to house the collection of equipment because of its clear weather, low relative humidity, and steady atmosphere. Eight different astronomical research institutions maintain and operate the telescopes. The observatory is overseen by the National Optical Astronomy Observatories. One of the most prominent telescopes housed at Kitt Peak is the McMath-Pierce Solar Telescope, the second-largest solar telescope in the world.

united states' largest collections of telescopes

number of telescopes

21	13	13	8	7
Kitt Peak National Observatory, Arizona	Custer Institute, New York	Mauna Kea, Hawaii	Stull Observatory, New York	Lick Observatory, California

state that grows the most rice

Arkansas

Farmers in Arkansas produced 5.78 million tons (5.2 million t) of rice in 2010, which was more than 47 percent of all rice grown in the country. With that harvest, farmers could give every person in the United States 36 pounds (16 kg) of rice and still have a little left over. There are more than 1.59 million acres (634,450 ha) of rice planted across the state, and the crops bring about $1.33 billion in revenue annually. Agriculture is a very important part of Arkansas's economy, employing more than 287,000 workers, or about 20 percent of the state's workforce.

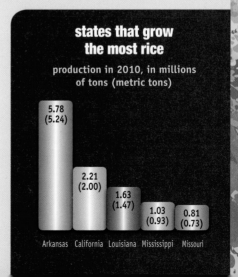

states that grow the most rice

production in 2010, in millions of tons (metric tons)

Arkansas	California	Louisiana	Mississippi	Missouri
5.78 (5.24)	2.21 (2.00)	1.63 (1.47)	1.03 (0.93)	0.81 (0.73)

Kobe Bryant,
Los Angeles Lakers

state with the most pro sports teams
California

With 19 professional teams across the state, California leads the nation in sports franchises. The state's five baseball teams include the LA Angels, the LA Dodgers, the San Diego Padres, the Oakland A's, and the San Francisco Giants. California also has five basketball teams, including the NBA's LA Lakers, LA Clippers, Sacramento Kings, Golden State Warriors, and the WNBA's LA Sparks. The Anaheim Ducks, the LA Kings, and the San Jose Sharks are the hockey teams that call the state home. The NFL is represented in California by the Oakland Raiders, San Francisco 49ers, and the San Diego Chargers. Finally, the state's soccer teams include the San Jose Earthquakes, the LA Galaxy, and the Chivas USA.

states with the most pro sports teams

number of professional baseball, basketball, football, hockey, and soccer teams

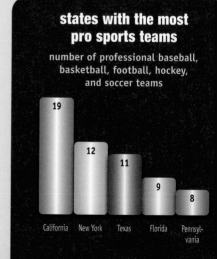

California	New York	Texas	Florida	Pennsylvania
19	12	11	9	8

state with the tallest sand dunes
Colorado

Star Dune, located in Great Sand Dunes National Park near Mosca, Colorado, is 750 feet (229 m) tall. That's almost five times taller than the Statue of Liberty! The park's dunes were formed from sand left behind by evaporated lakes. Wind picked up the sand and funneled it through the surrounding mountains until it collected in low-lying region. Visitors to the park are allowed to ski, sled, or slide down the giant dunes; this works best after a light rain. Many animals also call this park home, including pika, marmots, black bears, and mountain lions.

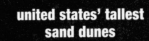

united states' tallest sand dunes

height, in feet (meters)

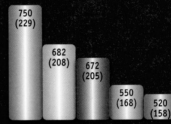

Great Sand Dunes, Colorado	Eureka Dunes, California	Kelso Dunes, California	Oregon Dunes, California	Sand Mountain, Nevada
750 (229)	682 (208)	672 (205)	550 (168)	520 (158)

US records

state with the oldest theme park
Connecticut

Lake Compounce in Bristol, Connecticut, first opened as a picnic park in 1846. The park's first electric roller coaster, the Green Dragon, was introduced in 1914 and cost ten cents per ride. It was replaced by the Wildcat in 1927, and the wooden coaster still operates today. In 1996 the park got a $50 million upgrade, which included the thrilling new roller coaster Boulder Dash. It is the only coaster to be built into a mountainside. Another $3.3 million was spent on upgrades in 2005, including an 800-foot (244 m) lazy river.

united states'
oldest theme parks
number of years open*

Lake Compounce, Connecticut (1846)	Cedar Point, Ohio (1870)	Idlewild Park, Pennsylvania (1878)	Seabreeze Park, New York (1879)	Lakemont Park, Pennsylvania (1894)
165	141	133	132	117

*As of 2011

state with the largest pumpkin-throwing contest
Delaware

Each year approximately 20,000 people gather in Sussex County, Delaware, for the annual World Championship Punkin Chunkin. More than 72 teams compete during the three-day festival to see who can chuck their pumpkin the farthest. Each team constructs a machine that has a mechanical or compressed-air firing device—no explosives are allowed. The farthest a pumpkin has traveled during the championship is 4,434 feet (1,352 m), or the length of twelve football fields. The 2010 competition grossed more than $100,000, and more than $70,000 of it was donated to local scholarship funds. The first Punkin Chunkin competition was held in 1986.

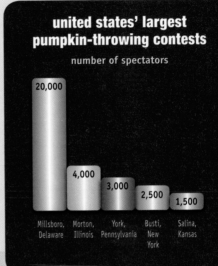

united states' largest pumpkin-throwing contests

number of spectators

Millsboro, Delaware	Morton, Illinois	York, Pennsylvania	Busti, New York	Salina, Kansas
20,000	4,000	3,000	2,500	1,500

state with the most lightning strikes

Florida

Southern Florida is known as the Lightning Capital of the United States, with 26.3 bolts occurring over each square mile (2.6 sq km)—the equivalent of ten city blocks—each year. Some 70 percent of all strikes occur between noon and 6:00 p.m., and the most dangerous months are July and August. Most lightning bolts measure 2 to 3 miles (5.2 to 7.8 km) long and can generate between 100 million and 1 billion volts of electricity. The air in a lightning bolt is heated to 50,000°F (27,760°C).

states with the most lightning strikes

annual bolts per square mile (2.6 sq k

Florida	Louisiana	Mississippi	Alabama	South Carolina
26.3	21.1	18.4	16.5	14.8

state with the largest sports hall of fame
Georgia

The Georgia Sports Hall of Fame fills 43,000 square feet (3,995 sq m) with memorabilia from Georgia's most accomplished college, amateur, and professional athletes. Some 230,000 bricks, 245 tons (222 t) of steel, and 7,591 pounds (3,443 kg) of glass were used in its construction. The hall owns more than 3,000 artifacts and displays about 1,000 of them at a time. Some Hall of Famers include baseball legend Hank Aaron, Olympic basketball great Theresa Edwards, and Super Bowl I champion Bill Curry.

united states' largest sports halls of fame

area, in square feet (square meters)

Georgia Sports Hall of Fame	Virginia Sports Hall of Fame	Alabama Sports Hall of Fame	Mississippi Sports Hall of Fame	Kansas Sports Hall of Fame
43,000 (3,995)	35,000 (3,000)	33,000 (3,066)	21,542 (2,001)	21,000 (1,900)

state with the world's largest submillimeter wavelength telescope

Hawaii

Mauna Kea—located on the island of Hawaii—is home to the world's largest submillimeter wavelength telescope, with a diameter of 49 feet (15 m). The James Clerk Maxwell Telescope (JCMT) is used to study our solar system, interstellar dust and gas, and distant galaxies. Mauna Kea also houses one of the world's largest optical/infrared (Keck I and II) and dedicated infrared (UKIRT) telescopes in the world. Mauna Kea is an ideal spot for astronomy because the atmosphere above the dormant volcano is very dry with little cloud cover, and its distance from city lights ensures a clear night sky.

world's largest submillime wavelength telescopes

diameter of lens, in feet (meters

James Clerk Maxwell Telescope (JCMT), Hawaii, USA	Caltech Submilli-meter Observatory (CSO), Hawaii, USA	Atacama Submilli-meter Telescope (ASTE), Chile	Heinrich Hertz Telescope (HHT), Arizona, USA	Submilli-meter Telescope (SMT), Arizona, USA
49.0 (15.0)	34.0 (10.4)	32.8 (10.0)	32.8 (10.0)	32.8 (10.0)

state with the largest human-made geyser

Idaho

The human-made geyser located in Soda Springs, Idaho, shoots water 150 feet (45.7 m) into the air. The geyser was created in November 1937 when people were searching for a hot water source for a thermal-heated swimming pool. The drill dug down about 315 feet (96 m) before it hit water. The pressure—created as water mixes with carbon dioxide gas—causes the water to shoot into the air. The Soda Springs geyser is now capped and controlled by a timer programmed to erupt every hour.

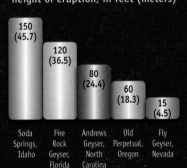

united states' largest human-made geysers

height of eruption, in feet (meters)

Soda Springs, Idaho	Fire Rock Geyser, Florida	Andrews Geyser, North Carolina	Old Perpetual, Oregon	Fly Geyser, Nevada
150 (45.7)	120 (36.5)	80 (24.4)	60 (18.3)	15 (4.5)

state with the tallest building
Illinois

The Willis Tower in Chicago, Illinois, is the tallest building in the western hemisphere at 1,451 feet (442 m). It is the ninth-tallest building in the world. Rising 110 stories above the pavement, the building offers about 3.8 million square feet (353,031 sq m) of retail and office space. The building, which was completed in 1973 as the Sears Tower, cost more than $150 million to build. It has a sky deck that offers visitors a view from the 103rd floor. On a clear day, people can see about 50 miles (80 km) into the surrounding states of Indiana, Wisconsin, and Michigan.

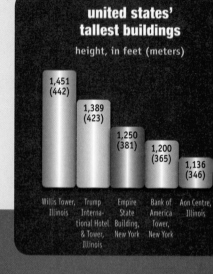

united states' tallest buildings
height, in feet (meters)

Willis Tower, Illinois	Trump International Hotel & Tower, Illinois	Empire State Building, New York	Bank of America Tower, New York	Aon Centre, Illinois
1,451 (442)	1,389 (423)	1,250 (381)	1,200 (365)	1,136 (346)

state with the largest half marathon

Indiana

Cars aren't the only things racing in Indianapolis, Indiana. Each May some 35,000 runners take part in the OneAmerica 500 Festival Mini-Marathon. This makes the mini-marathon the nation's largest half marathon and the nation's eighth-longest road race. The 13.1-mile (21.1 km) race winds through downtown and includes a lap along the Indianapolis Motor Speedway oval. About 100 musical groups entertain the runners as they complete the course. A giant pasta dinner and after-race party await the runners at the end of the day. The mini-marathon is part of a weekend celebration that centers around the Indianapolis 500 auto race.

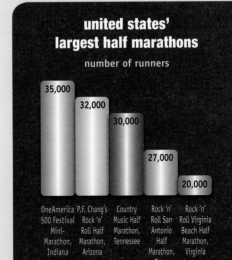

**united states'
largest half marathons**

number of runners

35,000	OneAmerica 500 Festival Mini-Marathon, Indiana
32,000	P.F. Chang's Rock 'n' Roll Half Marathon, Arizona
30,000	Country Music Half Marathon, Tennessee
27,000	Rock 'n' Roll San Antonio Half Marathon, Texas
20,000	Rock 'n' Roll Virginia Beach Half Marathon, Virginia

state with the highest egg production

Iowa

Iowa tops all other states in the country in egg production, turning out more than 14.6 billion eggs per year. That's enough to give every person in the United States about three and a half dozen eggs each! That's a good thing, because each person in America eats about 248 eggs per year. The state has 57 million laying hens, and each is capable of laying about 254 eggs a year. These hungry hens eat about 55 million bushels of corn and 27.5 million bushels of soybeans annually. In addition to selling the eggs as they are, Iowa's processing plants turn them into frozen, liquid, dried, or specialty egg products.

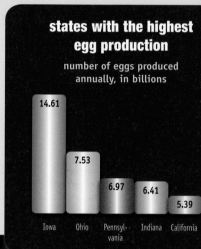

states with the highest egg production

number of eggs produced annually, in billions

Iowa	Ohio	Pennsyl-vania	Indiana	California
14.61	7.53	6.97	6.41	5.39

state with the windiest city

Kansas

According to average annual wind speeds collected by the National Climatic Data Center, Dodge City, Kansas, is the windiest city in the United States, with an average wind speed of 14 miles (22.5 km) per hour. Located in Ford County, the city borders the Santa Fe Trail and is rich in history. The city was founded in 1872 and had a reputation as a tough cowboy town. With help from legendary sheriffs like Wyatt Earp, order was established and the town grew steadily. Today tourists come to take in the area's history.

united states' windiest cities

average wind speed, in miles (kilometers) per hour

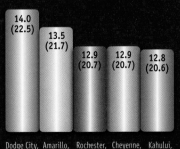

Dodge City, Kansas	Amarillo, Texas	Rochester, Minnesota	Cheyenne, Wyoming	Kahului, Hawaii
14.0 (22.5)	13.5 (21.7)	12.9 (20.7)	12.9 (20.7)	12.8 (20.6)

state with the most popular horse race
Kentucky

Each year, the Kentucky Derby draws more than 155,000 people who gather to watch "the most exciting two minutes in sports." The race is run at Churchill Downs in Louisville, on a dirt track that measures 1.25 miles (2 km) long. The thoroughbred horses must be three years old to race, and the winner nabs a $2 million purse. The winning horse is covered in a blanket of 554 red roses, which gave the race the nickname "The Run for the Roses." The fastest horse to complete the race was Secretariat in 1973, with a time of 1:59:40.

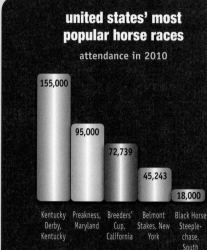

united states' most popular horse races
attendance in 2010

155,000	95,000	72,739	45,243	18,000
Kentucky Derby, Kentucky	Preakness, Maryland	Breeders' Cup, California	Belmont Stakes, New York	Black Horse Steeple-chase, South Carolina

Secretariat

GATOR XING
NEXT 1/2 MILE

state with the largest alligator population
Louisiana

There are approximately 2 million alligators living in Louisiana. About 1.5 million alligators live in the wild, and another half million are raised on farms. In 1986, Louisiana began an alligator ranching business, which encourages farmers to raise thousands of the reptiles each year. The farmers must return some alligators to the wild, but they are allowed to sell the rest for profit. The released alligators have an excellent chance of thriving in the wild because they have been well fed and are a good size. Although alligators can be found in the state's bayous, swamps, and ponds, most live in Louisiana's 3 million acres (1.2 million ha) of coastal marshland.

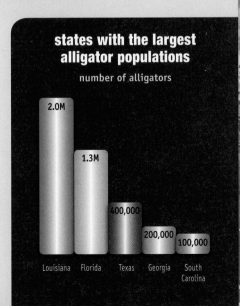

states with the largest alligator populations
number of alligators

2.0M — Louisiana
1.3M — Florida
400,000 — Texas
200,000 — Georgia
100,000 — South Carolina

state with the oldest state fair

Maine

The first Skowhegan State Fair took place in 1819—a year before Maine officially became a state! The fair took place in January, and hundreds of people came despite the harsh weather. Originally sponsored by the Somerset Central Agricultural Society, the fair name became official in 1842. State fairs were very important in the 1800s. With no agricultural colleges in existence, fairs became the best way for farmers to learn about new agricultural methods and equipment. Today the Skowhegan State Fair features more than 7,000 exhibitors who compete for prize money totaling more than $200,000. The fair also includes a demolition derby, a children's barnyard, concerts, livestock exhibits, and arts and crafts.

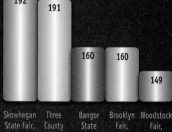

united states' oldest state fairs

number of years since fair first held*

Skowhegan State Fair, Maine (1819)	Three County Fair, Massachu-setts (1820)	Bangor State Fair, Maine (1851)	Brooklyn Fair, Connecti-cut (1851)	Woodstock Fair, Vermont (1862)
192	191	160	160	149

*As of 2011

College Park Aviation Museum

state with the oldest airport
Maryland

The Wright brothers founded College Park Airport in 1909 to teach army officers how to fly, and it has been in operation ever since. The airport is now owned by the Maryland-National Capital Park and Planning Commission and is on the Register of Historic Places. Many aviation "firsts" occurred at this airport, such as the first woman passenger in the United States (1909), the first test of a bomb-dropping device (1911), and the first US airmail service (1918). The College Park Aviation Museum is located on its grounds, and it exhibits aviation memorabilia.

united states' oldest airports
number of years open*

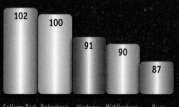

College Park Airport, Maryland (1909)	Robertson Airport, Connecticut (1911)	Hartness State Airport, Vermont (1920)	Middlesboro-Bell County Airport, Kentucky (1921)	Page Field, Florida (1924)
102	100	91	90	87

*As of 2011

state with the oldest baseball stadium

Massachusetts

Fenway Park opened its doors to Massachusetts baseball fans on April 20, 1912. The Boston Red Sox—the park's home team—won the World Series that year. The park celebrated in 2004 when the Sox won the World Series again. The park is also the home of the Green Monster—a giant 37-foot (11.3 m) wall with an additional 23-foot (7 m) screen that has plagued home-run hitters since the park first opened. The park's unique dimensions were not intended to prevent home runs, however; they were meant to keep nonpaying fans outside. A seat out in the right-field bleachers is painted red to mark where the longest measurable home run hit inside the park landed. It measured 502 feet (153 m) and was hit by Ted Williams in 1946. Some of the other baseball legends who played at Fenway include Cy Young, Babe Ruth, Jimmie Fox, and Carlton Fisk.

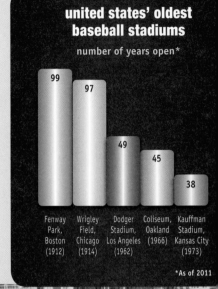

united states' oldest baseball stadiums

number of years open*

Fenway Park, Boston (1912)	Wrigley Field, Chicago (1914)	Dodger Stadium, Los Angeles (1962)	Coliseum, Oakland (1966)	Kauffman Stadium, Kansas City (1973)
99	97	49	45	38

*As of 2011

BOSTON RED SOX

state with the largest stadium
Michigan

Michigan Stadium—also known as the Big House—is the home of the University of Michigan Wolverines, and can hold 109,901 football fans during the home games. The stadium was constructed in 1927 using 440 tons (399 t) of reinforcing steel and 31,000 square feet (2,880 sq m) of wire mesh to create a 82,000-seat venue. After several renovations, the stadium reached its current seating capacity in 2010. The most recent additions include luxury boxes and club seating. Since its inaugural game, Michigan Stadium has hosted more than 35 million fans.

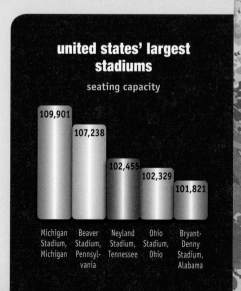

united states' largest stadiums
seating capacity

Stadium	Seating Capacity
Michigan Stadium, Michigan	109,901
Beaver Stadium, Pennsylvania	107,238
Neyland Stadium, Tennessee	102,455
Ohio Stadium, Ohio	102,329
Bryant-Denny Stadium, Alabama	101,821

state with the largest indoor theme park

Minnesota

Nickelodeon Universe is located inside the Mall of America in Bloomington, Minnesota, and covers 7 acres (2.8 ha). The park offers 30 rides, including the Xcel Energy Log Chute, SpongeBob SquarePants Rock Bottom Plunge, Splat-O-Sphere, Skyscraper Ferris wheel, Timber Twister roller coaster, Mighty Axe, and Avatar Airbender. Some of the other attractions at the park are a rock-climbing wall, petting zoo, and game arcade. Kids can also meet Dora, Diego, Blue, and SpongeBob.

united states' largest indoor theme parks

area, in acres (hectares)

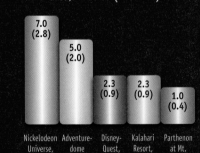

7.0 (2.8)	5.0 (2.0)	2.3 (0.9)	2.3 (0.9)	1.0 (0.4)
Nickelodeon Universe, Minnesota	Adventure-dome Theme Park, Nevada	Disney-Quest, Florida	Kalahari Resort, Wisconsin	Parthenon at Mt. Olympus, Wisconsin

state with the most catfish
Mississippi

There are about 388 million catfish in Mississippi—more than 60 percent of the world's farm-raised supply. That's almost enough to give every person in the state 132 fish each. There are about 80,200 water acres (32,000 ha) used to farm catfish in Mississippi. The state's residents are quite proud of their successful fish industry and celebrate at the World Catfish Festival in Belzoni.

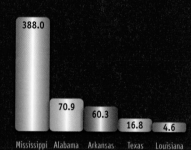

states with the most catfish

number of catfish, in millions

Mississippi	Alabama	Arkansas	Texas	Louisiana
388.0	70.9	60.3	16.8	4.6

US records

state with the largest outdoor theater
Missouri

The Municipal Theatre in St. Louis, Missouri—affectionately known as the Muny—is the nation's largest outdoor theater, with 80,000 square feet (7,432 sq m) and 11,500 seats—about the same size as a regulation soccer field. Amazingly, construction for the giant theater was completed in just 42 days at a cost of $10,000. The theater opened in 1917 with a production of Verdi's *Aïda*, and the best seats cost only $1. The Muny offers classic Broadway shows each summer, with past productions including *The King and I*, *The Wizard of Oz*, and *Oliver!* The last nine rows of the theater are always held as free seats for the public, just as they have been since the Muny opened.

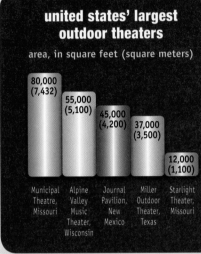

united states' largest outdoor theaters

area, in square feet (square meters)

80,000 (7,432)	55,000 (5,100)	45,000 (4,200)	37,000 (3,500)	12,000 (1,100)
Municipal Theatre, Missouri	Alpine Valley Music Theater, Wisconsin	Journal Pavilion, New Mexico	Miller Outdoor Theater, Texas	Starlight Theater, Missouri

state with the largest bighorn sheep population
Montana

With a population of about 5,700 bighorn sheep, Montana has more of these wild endangered mammals than any other state. The population has quadrupled in the last 60 years. Many of Montana's bighorn sheep live in an area known as the Rocky Mountain Front—a 100-mile (160.9 km) area that stretches from Glacier National Park to the town of Lincoln. A ram's horns can weigh up to 30 pounds (13.6 kg)—more than all of the bones in its body. Rams use these giant horns when they butt heads with a rival, and can hit each other at up to 20 miles (32.2 km) per hour.

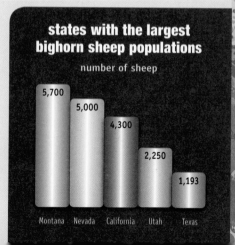

states with the largest bighorn sheep populations
number of sheep

Montana	Nevada	California	Utah	Texas
5,700	5,000	4,300	2,250	1,193

state with the largest hailstone
Nebraska

During a severe thunderstorm on June 22, 2003, the small town of Aurora, Nebraska, was pounded with a hailstone that measured at least 7 inches (17.8 cm) in diameter and had a circumference of 18.8 inches (47.7 cm). That's about the same size as a soccer ball. Scientists think that the hailstone was probably even bigger, but had melted some before it was preserved in a freezer. Hailstones of this size can fall at a speed of 100 miles (161 km) an hour. Sometimes hailstones can contain other objects, such as rocks, insects, and leaves.

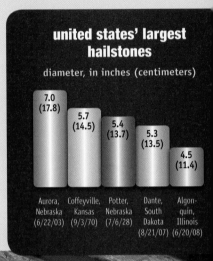

united states' largest hailstones

diameter, in inches (centimeters)

7.0 (17.8)	5.7 (14.5)	5.4 (13.7)	5.3 (13.5)	4.5 (11.4)
Aurora, Nebraska (6/22/03)	Coffeyville, Kansas (9/3/70)	Potter, Nebraska (7/6/28)	Dante, South Dakota (8/21/07)	Algonquin, Illinois (6/20/08)

state with the largest glass sculpture
Nevada

Fiori di Como—the breathtaking chandelier at the Bellagio Hotel in Las Vegas, Nevada—measures 65.7 feet by 29.5 feet (20 m by 9 m). Created by Dale Chihuly, the handblown glass chandelier consists of more than 2,000 discs of colored glass. Each disc is about 18 inches (45.7 cm) wide and hangs about 20 feet (6.1 m) overhead. Together, these colorful discs look like a giant field of flowers. The chandelier required about 10,000 pounds (4,536 kg) of steel and 40,000 pounds (18,144 kg) of handblown glass. The sculpture's name translates to "Flowers of Como." The Bellagio was modeled after the hotel on Lake Como in Italy.

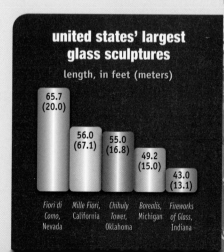

united states' largest glass sculptures
length, in feet (meters)

Fiori di Como, Nevada	Mille Fiori, California	Chihuly Tower, Oklahoma	Borealis, Michigan	Fireworks of Glass, Indiana
65.7 (20.0)	56.0 (67.1)	55.0 (16.8)	49.2 (15.0)	43.0 (13.1)

state with the oldest lottery

New Hampshire

New Hampshire was the first state to establish a legal lottery system when it sold its first ticket in 1964. The lottery was originally established to raise money for charitable causes throughout the state. Since it began, the New Hampshire Lottery has seen more than $4.1 billion in sales and other earnings—about $2.7 billion was paid out as prize money, and about $1.3 billion has gone to fund education in the state. The main in-state lottery in New Hampshire is called the Weekly Grand, but residents also participate in several multistate lotteries as well.

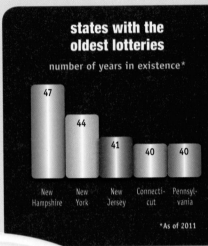

states with the oldest lotteries

number of years in existence*

New Hampshire	New York	New Jersey	Connecticut	Pennsylvania
47	44	41	40	40

*As of 2011

state with the world's longest boardwalk
New Jersey

The famous boardwalk in Atlantic City, New Jersey, stretches for 4 miles (6.4 km) along the beach. Combined with the adjoining boardwalk in Ventnor, the length increases to just under 6 miles (9.7 km). The 60-foot (18 m) wide boardwalk opened on June 26, 1870. It was the first boardwalk built in the United States, and was designed to keep sand out of the tourists' shoes. Today the boardwalk is filled with amusement parks, shops, restaurants, and hotels. The boardwalk recently received a $100 million face-lift, which included new roofs, signs, and storefronts for surrounding buildings. About 37 million people take a stroll along the walk each year.

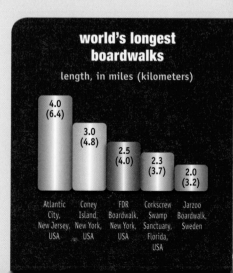

world's longest boardwalks
length, in miles (kilometers)

Atlantic City, New Jersey, USA	Coney Island, New York, USA	FDR Boardwalk, New York, USA	Corkscrew Swamp Sanctuary, Florida, USA	Jarzoo Boardwalk, Sweden
4.0 (6.4)	3.0 (4.8)	2.5 (4.0)	2.3 (3.7)	2.0 (3.2)

state with the largest balloon festival
New Mexico

During the 2010 Kodak Albuquerque International Balloon Fiesta in New Mexico, approximately 500 hot-air and gas-filled balloons sailed across the sky. Held each October, the fiesta draws more than 760,000 spectators. This event attracts balloons from around the world, and is often seen in more than 50 countries. The festival takes place in the 200-acre (81 ha) Balloon Fiesta State Park. The Balloon Fiesta has also hosted some prestigious balloon races, including the Gordon Bennett Cup (1993), the World Gas Balloon Championship (1994), and the America's Challenge Gas Balloon Race (2006).

united states' largest balloon festivals

approximate number of balloons

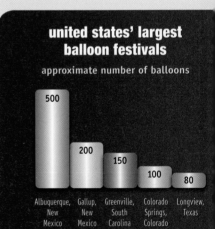

500	200	150	100	80
Albuquerque, New Mexico	Gallup, New Mexico	Greenville, South Carolina	Colorado Springs, Colorado	Longview, Texas

state with the longest underwater tunnel

New York

The Brooklyn-Battery Tunnel in New York measures 1.73 miles (2.78 km) long, making it the longest underwater tunnel in North America and the longest continuous underwater vehicular tunnel in the world. The tunnel passes under the East River and connects Battery Park in Manhattan with the Red Hook section of Brooklyn. It took 13,900 tons (12,609 t) of steel, about 205,000 cubic yards (156,700 cu m) of concrete, approximately 1,871 miles (3,011 km) of electrical wire, some 883,391 bolts, and 799,000 wall and ceiling tiles to build the tunnel. Completed in 1950, the $90-million tunnel carries about 60,000 vehicles a day.

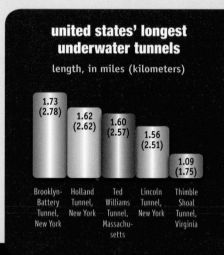

united states' longest underwater tunnels

length, in miles (kilometers)

Tunnel	Length
Brooklyn-Battery Tunnel, New York	1.73 (2.78)
Holland Tunnel, New York	1.62 (2.62)
Ted Williams Tunnel, Massachusetts	1.60 (2.57)
Lincoln Tunnel, New York	1.56 (2.51)
Thimble Shoal Tunnel, Virginia	1.09 (1.75)

state that grows the most sweet potatoes

North Carolina

North Carolina leads the country in sweet potato production, growing about 972 million pounds (440 kg) each year. This accounts for more than 41 percent of the nation's sweet potato production. Farmers plant about 55,000 acres (22,257 ha) of sweet potato plants annually. In fact, the sweet potato is the official state vegetable of North Carolina. Oddly enough, these sweet veggies aren't really potatoes at all. Sweet potatoes are root plants—not tubers—and are actually part of the morning glory family.

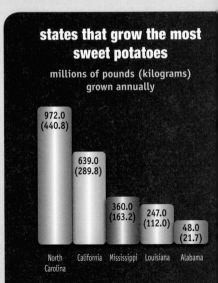

states that grow the most sweet potatoes

millions of pounds (kilograms) grown annually

North Carolina	972.0 (440.8)
California	639.0 (289.8)
Mississippi	360.0 (163.2)
Louisiana	247.0 (112.0)
Alabama	48.0 (21.7)

state with the tallest metal sculpture

North Dakota

In August 2001, Gary Greff created a 110-foot (33.5 m) tall metal sculpture along the stretch of road between Gladstone and Regent, North Dakota. That's the height of an 11-story building! The 154-foot (46.9 m) wide sculpture is called *Geese in Flight*, and shows Canada geese traveling across the prairie. Greff has created several other towering sculptures nearby, and the road has become known as the Enchanted Highway. He created these sculptures to attract tourists to the area and to support his hometown. He relies only on donations to finance his work.

united states' tallest metal sculptures

height, in feet (meters)

Geese in Flight, North Dakota	Deer Crossing, North Dakota	Bass Fish, North Dakota	Egyptian Longhorn, South Dakota	Needle Tower, Oregon
110 (33.5)	75 (22.9)	70 (21.3)	60 (18.3)	60 (18.3)

state with the world's largest twins gathering

Ohio

Each August, the town of Twinsburg, Ohio, hosts more than 3,400 twins at its annual Twins Day Festival. Both identical and fraternal twins from around the world participate, and many dress alike. The twins take part in games and contests, such as the oldest identical twins and the twins with the widest combined smile. There is also a Double Take parade, which is nationally televised. There are special twin programs for all age groups, since twins from ages 90 years to just 11 days old have attended. The event began in 1976 in honor of Aaron and Moses Wilcox, twin brothers who inspired the city to adopt its name in 1817.

world's largest twins gatherings

number of attendees

3,400	2,500	2,000	2,000	1,500
Twins Day Festival, Ohio, USA	Twins Weekend, Canada	"Deux et plus" Gathering, France	Montreal Canada Twins Festival, Canada	Twins Plus Festival, Australia

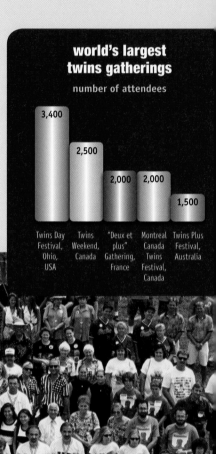

state with the world's longest multiple-arch dam

Oklahoma

With a length of 6,565 feet (2,001 m), the Pensacola Dam in Oklahoma is the world's longest multiple-arch dam. Built in 1940, the dam is located on the Grand River and contains the Grand Lake o' the Cherokees—one of the largest reservoirs in the country with 46,500 surface acres (18,818 ha) of water. The dam stands 145 feet (44 m) high. It was made out of 535,000 cubic yards of concrete, some 655,000 barrels of cement, another 10 million pounds (4.5 million kg) of structural steel, and 75,000 pounds (340,194 kg) of copper. The dam cost $27 million to complete.

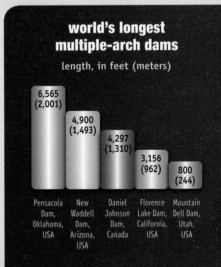

world's longest multiple-arch dams

length, in feet (meters)

Dam	Length
Pensacola Dam, Oklahoma, USA	6,565 (2,001)
New Waddell Dam, Arizona, USA	4,900 (1,493)
Daniel Johnson Dam, Canada	4,297 (1,310)
Florence Lake Dam, California, USA	3,156 (962)
Mountain Dell Dam, Utah, USA	800 (244)

state with the deepest lake

Oregon

At a depth of 1,932 feet (589 m), Crater Lake in southern Oregon partially fills the remains of an old volcanic basin. The crater was formed almost 7,700 years ago when Mount Mazama erupted and then collapsed. The lake averages about 5 miles (8 km) in diameter. Crater Lake National Park—the nation's fifth-oldest park—surrounds the majestic lake and measures 249 square miles (645 sq km). The area's large snowfalls average 530 inches (1,346 cm) a year, and supply Crater Lake with its water. In addition to being the United States' deepest lake, it's also the eighth-deepest lake in the world.

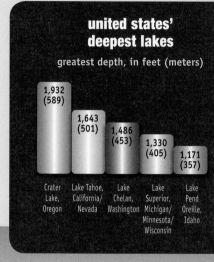

united states' deepest lakes

greatest depth, in feet (meters)

1,932 (589)	1,643 (501)	1,486 (453)	1,330 (405)	1,171 (357)
Crater Lake, Oregon	Lake Tahoe, California/ Nevada	Lake Chelan, Washington	Lake Superior, Michigan/ Minnesota/ Wisconsin	Lake Pend Oreille, Idaho

state with the oldest drive-in theater
Pennsylvania

Shankweiler's Drive-in Theater opened in 1934. It was the country's second drive-in theater, and is the oldest one still operating today. Located in Orefield, Pennsylvania, the single-screen theater can accommodate 320 cars. Approximately 90 percent of the theater's guests are children. Although they originally used sound boxes located beside the cars, today's patrons can tune into a special radio station to hear the movies' music and dialogue. Shankweiler's is open from April to September.

united states' oldest drive-in theaters
number of years open*

Shank- weiler's Drive-in Theater, Pennsyl- vania (1934)	Lynn Auto Theatre, Ohio (1937)	Saco Drive-in, Maine (1939)	Hiway 50 Drive-in Theater, Tennessee (1946)	Sunset Drive-in Theater, Pennsyl- vania (1948)
77	74	72	65	63

*As of 2011

US records

state with the oldest temple
Rhode Island

The Touro Synagogue was dedicated during Hanukkah in December 1763 and is the oldest temple in the United States. Located in Newport, Rhode Island, the temple was designed by famous architect Peter Harrison and took four years to complete. In addition to serving as a symbol of religious freedom, the temple played another part in the country's history. When the British captured Newport in 1776, the temple briefly became a British hospital. Then, in 1781, George Washington met General Lafayette there to plan the final battles of the Revolution.

united states' oldest temples

number of years since dedication*

Temple	Years
Touro Synagogue, Rhode Island (1763)	248
B'nai Jeshurun, New York (1825)	186
Kahal Kadosh Beth Elohim Synagogue, South Carolina (1841)	170
Shul of New York, New York (1849)	162
Ohev Sholom Talmud Torah, District of Columbia (1886)	125

*As of 2011

state with the oldest museum

South Carolina

The Charleston Museum in Charleston, South Carolina, was founded in 1773—three years before the Declaration of Independence was signed. The museum was founded to preserve the culture and history of the southern town and the surrounding area, and opened its doors to the public in 1824. Some of the exhibits in the museum include furniture, silver, and art made in the area, as well as fossils of local birds and animals. Two historic houses, which were built between 1772 and 1803, are also run by the museum. Visitors can tour these homes to learn about the state's early architecture.

united states' oldest museums

number of years open*

Charleston Museum, South Carolina (1773)	Albany Institute of History & Art, New York (1791)	Peabody Essex Museum, Massachusetts (1799)	Peale Museum, Maryland (1814)	Pilgrim Hall, Massachusetts (1824)
238	220	212	197	187

*As of 2011

state with the largest petrified wood collection
South Dakota

Lemmon's Petrified Wood Park in South Dakota is home to 30 acres (12.1 ha) of petrified wood. It covers an entire city block in downtown Lemmon. It was built between 1930 and 1932 when locals collected petrified wood from the area and constructed displays. One structure in the park—known as the Castle—weighs more than 300 tons (272 t) and is made partly from petrified wood and partly of petrified dinosaur and mammoth bones. Other exhibits include a wishing well, a waterfall, the Lemmon Pioneer Museum, and hundreds of pile sculptures.

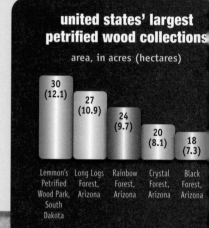

united states' largest petrified wood collections

area, in acres (hectares)

Lemmon's Petrified Wood Park, South Dakota	Long Logs Forest, Arizona	Rainbow Forest, Arizona	Crystal Forest, Arizona	Black Forest, Arizona
30 (12.1)	27 (10.9)	24 (9.7)	20 (8.1)	18 (7.3)

state with the world's largest freshwater aquarium

Tennessee

The Tennessee Aquarium in Chattanooga is an impressive 130,000 square feet (12,077 sq m), making it the largest freshwater aquarium in the world. The $45 million building holds a total of 400,000 gallons (1,514,165 L) of water. In addition, the aquarium features a 60,000-square-foot (5,574 sq m) building dedicated to the ocean and the creatures that live there. Permanent features in the aquarium include a discovery hall and an environmental learning lab. Some of the aquarium's 12,000 animals include baby alligators, paddlefish, lake sturgeon, sea dragons, and pipefish. And to feed all of these creatures, the aquarium goes through 12,000 crickets, 33,300 worms, and 1,200 pounds (545 kg) of seafood each month!

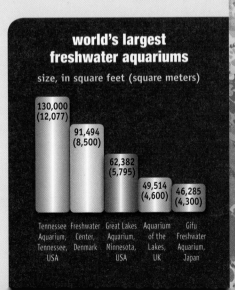

world's largest freshwater aquariums

size, in square feet (square meters)

130,000 (12,077)	Tennessee Aquarium, Tennessee, USA
91,494 (8,500)	Freshwater Center, Denmark
62,382 (5,795)	Great Lakes Aquarium, Minnesota, USA
49,514 (4,600)	Aquarium of the Lakes, UK
46,285 (4,300)	Gifu Freshwater Aquarium, Japan

state with the biggest ferris wheel

Texas

The State Fair of Texas boasts the nation's largest Ferris wheel. Called the Texas Star, this colossal wheel measures 212 feet (64.6 m) high. That's taller than a 20-story building! The Texas Star was built in Italy and shipped to Texas for its debut at the 1986 fair. Located in the 277-acre (112 ha) Fair Park, the Texas Star is just one of the 70 rides featured at the fair. The three-week-long State Fair of Texas is the biggest state fair in the country and brings in about $350 million in revenue annually. It is held in the fall, and the giant Ferris wheel is not the only grand-scale item there. Big Tex, a 52-foot (15.9 m) tall cowboy, is the fair's mascot and the biggest cowboy in the United States.

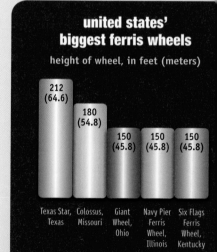

united states' biggest ferris wheels

height of wheel, in feet (meters)

Texas Star, Texas	Colossus, Missouri	Giant Wheel, Ohio	Navy Pier Ferris Wheel, Illinois	Six Flags Ferris Wheel, Kentucky
212 (64.6)	180 (54.8)	150 (45.8)	150 (45.8)	150 (45.8)

state with the largest dinosaur collection

Utah

The Museum of Ancient Life at the Thanksgiving Point Institute in Lehi, Utah, has the largest dinosaur collection in the country with 60 complete skeletons on display. Guests are even invited to touch some of the real fossils, bones, and eggs that they are looking at. There are about 50 interactive displays throughout the Museum of Ancient Life. Guests touring the museum can also observe a working paleontology lab. The museum, which opened in June 2000, holds a sleepover once a month for kids to go on a behind-the-scenes tour.

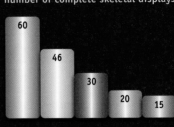

united states' largest dinosaur collections

number of complete skeletal displays

Museum of Ancient Life, Utah	Smith-sonian Museum of Natural History, District of Columbia	Rocky Mountain Dinosaur Research Center, Colorado	Wyoming Dinosaur Center, Wyoming	Academy of Natural Sciences, Pennsyl-vania
60	46	30	20	15

US records

state that produces the most maple syrup

Vermont

Maple syrup production in Vermont totaled 890,000 gallons (3,369,016 L) in 2010 and accounted for about 45 percent of the United States' total yield that year. There are approximately 3.2 million tree taps used by the state's 2,000 maple syrup producers, and the annual production generates almost $13.1 million. It takes about five tree taps to collect enough maple sap—approximately 40 gallons (151.4 L)—to produce just 1 gallon (3.79 L) of syrup. Vermont maple syrup is also made into maple sugar, maple cream, and maple candies.

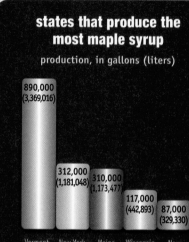

states that produce the most maple syrup

production, in gallons (liters)

Vermont	New York	Maine	Wisconsin	New Hampshire
890,000 (3,369,016)	312,000 (1,181,048)	310,000 (1,173,477)	117,000 (442,893)	87,000 (329,330)

state with the largest office building

Virginia

The Pentagon Building in Arlington, Virginia, measures 6,636,360 square feet (616,538 sq m) and covers 583 acres (236 ha). In fact, the US Capitol can fit inside the building five times! Although the Pentagon contains 17.5 miles (28.2 km) of hallways, the design of the building allows people to reach any destination in about seven minutes. The Pentagon is almost like a small city, employing about 23,000 people. About 200,000 phone calls are made there daily, and the internal post office handles about 1.2 million pieces of mail each month.

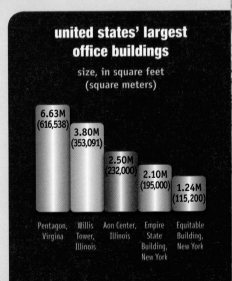

united states' largest office buildings

size, in square feet (square meters)

Building	Size
Pentagon, Virginia	6.63M (616,538)
Willis Tower, Illinois	3.80M (353,091)
Aon Center, Illinois	2.50M (232,000)
Empire State Building, New York	2.10M (195,000)
Equitable Building, New York	1.24M (115,200)

state with the longest train tunnel
Washington

The Cascade Tunnel runs through the Cascade Mountains in central Washington and measures 7.8 miles (12.6 km) long. The tunnel connects the towns of Berne and Scenic. It was built by the Great Northern Railway in 1929 to replace the original tunnel, which was built at an elevation frequently hit with snowslides. To help cool the trains' diesel engines and remove fumes, the tunnel is equipped with huge fans that blow air while and after a train passes.

united states' longest train tunnels

length, in miles (kilometers)

Cascade Tunnel, Washington	Flathead Tunnel, Missouri	Moffat Tunnel, Colorado	Hoosac Tunnel, Massachusetts	BART Transbay Tube, California
7.80 (12.60)	7.01 (12.50)	6.21 (10.00)	4.75 (7.56)	3.60 (5.79)

CASCADE TUNNEL
7.8 MILES LONG   ELEVATION 2,247 FEET
41,152 FEET LONG   COMPLETED 1928

state with the longest steel arch bridge
West Virginia

With a main span of 1,700 feet (518 m) and a weight of about 88 million pounds (40 million kg), the New River Gorge Bridge in Fayetteville, West Virginia, is the longest and largest steel arch bridge in the United States. It is approximately 875 feet (267 m) above the New River and is the second-highest bridge in the country. After three years of construction, the bridge was competed in 1977. The $37 million structure is the focus of Bridge Day—a statewide annual festival that is one of the largest extreme sports events in the United States, drawing hundreds of BASE jumpers and thousands of spectators.

united states' longest steel arch bridges

length of main span, in feet (meters)

Bridge	Length
New River Gorge Bridge, West Virginia	1,700 (518)
Bayonne Bridge, New Jersey	1,675 (511)
Fremont Bridge, Oregon	1,255 (383)
Roosevelt Lake Bridge, Arizona	1,080 (329)
Hell Gate Bridge, New York	1,038 (316)

state with the largest water park
Wisconsin

Noah's Ark in Wisconsin Dells, Wisconsin, sprawls for 70 acres (28.4 ha) and includes 49 waterslides. One of the most popular—Dark Voyage—takes visitors on a twisting rapids ride in the dark. The ride can pump 8,000 gallons (30,283 L) of water a minute. Visitors can also enjoy two wave pools, two mile-long "endless" rivers, and four children's play areas. It takes 5 million gallons (19 million L) of water— the equivalent of more than 14 Olympic-size swimming pools—to fill all the pools and operate the 3 miles (4.8 km) of waterslides. Noah's Ark also boasts the country's longest water coaster (Black Anaconda), the world's longest bowl ride (Time Warp), and the world's only 4-D drive-in theater.

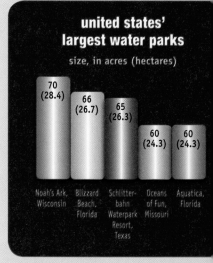

**united states'
largest water parks**

size, in acres (hectares)

70 (28.4)	66 (26.7)	65 (26.3)	60 (24.3)	60 (24.3)
Noah's Ark, Wisconsin	Blizzard Beach, Florida	Schlitterbahn Waterpark Resort, Texas	Oceans of Fun, Missouri	Aquatica, Florida

state with the world's largest outdoor rodeo

Wyoming

Cheyenne Frontier Days in Cheyenne, Wyoming, brings more than 550,000 spectators to the city during the last full week of July. The festival is not only the largest rodeo in the world but also the oldest continually running. Some 1,800 cowboys and cowgirls compete for the $1 million in prize money. Besides the rodeo, visitors enjoy entertainers, a free pancake breakfast for the first 10,000 diners, and the largest parade of horse-drawn antique carriages in the world. There is also the Western Art Show and Sale featuring more than 300 paintings, bronzes, and Navajo weavings.

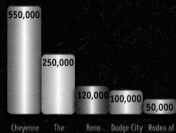

united states' largest outdoor rodeos

approximate annual attendance

550,000	250,000	120,000	100,000	50,000
Cheyenne Frontier Days, Wyoming	The Greeley Stampede, Colorado	Reno Rodeo, Nevada	Dodge City Rodeo, Kansas	Rodeo of the Ozarks, Arkansas

index

21, 41

A

A Chorus Line, 50
Aaron, Hank, 77, 79, 81, 86, 87
Abdul-Jabbar, Kareem, 56
AC/DC, 38, 46
Academy of Natural Science, 289
Action Comics, 215
Adele, 41
Adventuredome, 268
African bullfrog, 181
African elephant, 169, 173
Agassi, Andre, 91
Airlines, 240
"Airplanes," 36
Airports, 238, 239, 265
Akon, 39
Alabama, 246, 254, 267, 269, 278
Alabama Sports Hall of Fame, 255
Alaska, 204, 247
Alaskan king crab, 153
Albany Institute of History, 285
Albatross, 162, 166
Albuquerque, 276
Al-Deayea, Mohamed, 101
Alexander, Shaun, 65
Alice in Wonderland, 24
Alligator, 263
Allure of the Seas, 134
Alpine Valley Music Theater, 270
Amazing Race, The, 11
Amazon, 150
Amazon.com, 123
American Airlines, 240
American alligator, 183
American cockroach, 186

American Idol, 13
Amusement parks, 225, 234, 252, 268
Anaconda, 177
Andersen, Morten, 66
Anderson, Gary, 66
Anderson, Jasey-Jay, 116
Andrews Geyser, 257
Android, 129
Anguilla, 130
Aniston, Jennifer, 27
Anquetil, Jacques, 71
Anson, Capp, 87
Ant, 186
AOL, 121, 124
Aon Center, 258, 291
Apartments, 227
Apple, 128, 129
Apple.com, 123
Aquarium of the Lakes, 287
Aquatica, 294
Arabian Desert, 149
Arcaro, Eddie, 109
Arctic Ocean, 151
Arctic tern, 164
Argentina, 102
Arizona, 247, 248, 259, 281, 286, 293
Arkansas, 249, 269, 295
Armstrong, Duncan, 94
Armstrong, Lance, 71, 214
Asian elephant, 169
Ask, 124
Aswan, 195
Atacama submillimeter telescope, 256
Atlantic City, 275
Atlantic Ocean, 151
Augustus, Seimone, 57
Australia, 227, 280
Australian taipan, 178
Australian tiger beetle, 186
Autti, Antti, 116

Avatar, 24, 29, 31
AVE-S 103, 135

B

B.o.B, 36, 44
B'nai Jeshurun, 284
Baffin Island, 152
Bailey, Donovan, 96
Baiyoke Tower II, 229
Baker, Buddy, 104
Bald eagle, 165
Bangkok, 193
Bangladesh, 205
Bangor State Fair, 264
Bank of America Tower, 258
Barrow Island, 196
Barrymore, Drew, 19
BART Transbay Tube, 292
Baseball stadiums, 266
Basketball, 52–61, 219
Basking shark, 155
Bats, 174
Battery, 209
Baxter, Kenny, 20
Bay, Michael, 32
Baylor, Elgin, 53
Bayne, Trevor, 106
Bayonne Bridge, 293
BD-5J Microjet, 142
Beagle, 189
Bears, 168
Beatles, The, 38
Beaver, 170
Beaver Stadium, 232, 267
Becker, Boris, 91
Beckham, David, 99
Beijing Capital, 239
Belfour, Ed, 112
Bellagio Hotel, 273
Belmont Stakes, 262
Ben-Hur, 15
Bentley Continental Supersports, 139
Berra, Yogi, 82

Bettis, Jerome, 63
Beyoncé, 43
Biaggi, Max, 108
Bicycles, 214
Bieber, Justin, 34, 37
Big Pete, 136
Bigfin squid, 154
Bigfoot 5, 136
Bighorn sheep, 271
Billy Elliot, 49
Biltmore Hotel, 231
Bing, 124
Bird, 188
Black bear, 168
Black caiman, 183
Black Eyed Peas, The, 35, 40, 46
Black Forest, 286
Black Horse Steeplechase, 262
Black mamba, 178, 179
Black Widow, 136
Blanda, George, 66
Blind Side, The, 31
Blizzard Beach, 294
Blockbuster, 223
Bloom, Orlando, 20
Blue Flame, 138
Blue shark, 156, 158, 159
Blue whale, 160, 161
Blyleven, Bert, 78
BMW Isetta, 137
Boardwalks, 275
Bodyguard, The, 33
Boise National Forest, 247
Bolt, Usain, 96
Bon Jovi, 46
Bond, James, 25
Bonds, Barry, 76, 77, 81, 83, 87
"Boom Boom Pow," 40
Borealis, 273
Borg, Björn, 93
Borneo, 152
Boston Bruins, 110, 113

Boston Celtics, 52, 54
Boston Red Sox, 80, 84
Boston, 266
Boyle, Susan, 34
Brady, Tom, 69
Brazil, 102, 127, 238, 244
Breeders' Cup, 262
Bridges, 293
Broadway, 50
Brodeur, Martin, 112
Brooklyn Fair, 264
Brooklyn-Battery Tunnel, 277
Brooks & Dunn, 47
Bruckheimer, 32
Bryant, Kobe, 55
Bryant-Denny Stadium, 267
Bugatti Veyron 16.4 Super Sport, 139, 216
Buildings, 226, 227, 229, 230, 258, 291
Bull shark, 156
Bullock, Sandra, 27
Burger King, 222
Burj Al Arab, 229
Burj Khalifa, 230
Burnquist, Bob, 114, 115
Busch, Kyle, 106
Bushmaster, 178

C

Cactus, 197
California, 247–250, 260, 262, 271, 273, 278, 281, 282, 292
"California Gurls," 36, 44
California redwood, 198
Caltech Submillimeter Observatory, 256
Camel, 173
Cameron, James, 32
Campanella, Roy, 83
Canada, 238, 280, 281
Cane toad, 176
Capybara, 170
Carlton, Steve, 78, 85
Carney, John, 66
Carol Burnett Show, The, 10
Carrefour, 221
Carrey, Jim, 18
Cars, 137, 220, 241
Cascade Tunnel, 292
Caspian Sea, 148

Castor bean, 201
Cat, 188, 190
Catfish, 269
Cats, 50
Cayman Islands, 130
Cedar Point, 225, 252
Cell phones, 128–130, 212
Centipede, 186
Cephalopods, 154
Cerro el Cóndor, 147
Chamberlain, Wilt, 53, 56
Charleston Museum, 285
Checa, Carlos, 108
Cheers, 10
Cheetah, 172
Chesney, Kenny, 42
Chevrolet Silverado, 220
Cheyenne Frontier Days, 295
Chicago, 226, 236, 258, 266
Chicago Bears, 70
Chicago Bulls, 52
Chicago Cubs, 80
Chicago O'Hare International, 239
Chihuly Tower, 273
Chile, 203, 204, 231
China, 235, 241
Chinese giant salamander, 180
Chinstrap penguin, 163
Choi, Na Yeon, 73
Christie, Linford, 96
Chugach National Forest, 247
Cine Teatro Gran Rex, 233
Circle K, 223
Clemens, Roger, 78, 85
Clijsters, Kim, 90
Cobb, Ty, 79, 81, 86
Coco de mer, 202
Coconut, 202
Coconut crab, 153
Coliseum, 266
College Park Airport, 265
Colorado, 251, 276, 289, 292, 295
Colossal squid, 154
Colossus, 288
Combs, Sean (Diddy), 39

Comcast.net, 121
Comic books, 215
Common iguana, 182
Common krait, 179
Commonwealth Bay, 196
Concert tours, 46
Coney Island, 275
Connecticut, 60, 252, 264, 265, 274
Conrad, Lauren, 9
Cooper, Cynthia, 57
Corkscrew Swamp Sanctuary, 275
Corvette ZR1, 139
Cosgrove, Miranda, 8
Country music, 47
Country Music Half Marathon, 259
Cowboy Stadium, 228
Craigslist.com, 123
Crater Lake, 191
CRH3, 135
CRH380AL, 135
Cri-Cri, 142
Criminal Minds, 12
Cross, Marcia, 7
Cruise ships, 134
Crustaceans, 153
Crutchlow, Cal, 108
Cruz, Taio, 36
Cryer, Jon, 6
Crystal Forest, 286
Curitiba, 244
Custer Institute, 248
CVS, 221
Cycling, 71
Cyrus, Miley, 43

D

Daily Show with Jon Stewart, The, 11
Dallas Cowboys, 67, 218
Dallol, 193
Dams, 281
Daniel Johnson Dam, 281
Dark Knight, The, 23, 30
Davenport, Lindsay, 90
Davis, Bette, 16
Davis, Warwick, 20
Day, Pat, 109
De Araujo, Jr., Rodil, 114
De Coster, Roger, 107
Death Cap, 199
Deepwater Horizon, 206

Delaware, 253
Delta Air Lines, 240
Denmark, 125, 287
Denver Nuggets, 54
Depp, Johnny, 26
Desert locust, 187
Deserts, 149
Desperate Housewives, 7
Detroit Pistons, 52, 54
Detroit Red Wings, 110, 113
Devers, Gail, 97
Diamondback moth, 187
Diamonds, 145
Diaz, Cameron, 27
DiCaprio, Leonardo, 26
DiMaggio, Joe, 82
Dinosaurs, 289
Dionne, Marcel, 111
Disney's A Christmas Carol, 28
Disneyland, 225, 234
DisneyQuest, 268
Dodge City Rodeo, 295
Dodger Stadium, 266
Dodonpa, 133
Dog, 188, 189
Dolphin, 157
Domes, 228
Douglas fir, 198
Dr. Dre, 39
Dragonfly, 185
Drive-in theaters, 283
Ducati Desmosedici RR, 140
Duke, 61
Duncan, Tim, 55
Dunst, Kirsten, 19
Durant, Joe, 72
"Dynamite," 36

E

Eagles, The, 38
Earnhardt, Dale, 104, 105
Earthquakes, 204
eBay.com, 123
Eclipse 500, 142
Ecosse Titanium Series RR, 217
Edmonton Oilers, 110
Eggs, 260
El Guerrouj, Hicham, 89
Elliott, Bill, 104
Ellis, Greg, 20
Elway, John, 62
E-mail, 121

Emerson, Roy, 93
Eminem, 34–37, 41, 48
Emirates Crown, 227
Emperor penguin, 163, 166
Empire State Building, 258, 291
Emu, 166
Environmental issues, 244
Equitable Building, 291
Estadio Azteca, 232
Eucalyptus, 198
Eureka dunes, 251
Eureka, 192
Eureka Tower, 227
Eurocopter X3, 141
European salamander, 176
Evert, Chris, 92
Everts, Stefan, 107

F

Facebook, 122
Fairs, 264
Fame, The, 41
Fangs, 178
Fat Landy, 136
Faulk, Marshall, 65
Favre, Brett, 62
Fawcett, Joy, 100
FDR Boardwalk, 275
Fearless, 41
Federer, Roger, 91, 93
Fenway Park, 266
Ferrari 599 GTO, 139
Ferrari World, 133
Ferris wheel, 288
FIFA Soccer II, 118
Fin whale, 160, 161
Finding Nemo, 22
Fiori di Como, 273
Fire Rock Geyser, 257
Fire-bellied toad, 176
Fireworks of Glass, 273
Flathead Tunnel, 292
Flood, 205
Florence Lake Dam, 281
Florida, 250, 254, 263, 265, 268, 275, 294
Flower, 200
Fly Geyser, 257
Ford F-Series, 220
Forest cobra, 179
Forrest Gump, 33
Formula Rossa, 133
Foudy, Julie, 100

Four Seasons, 211
Fox Theatre, 233
Foxx, Jimmie, 82
France, 235, 280
Franchises, 222, 223
Francis, Ron, 111
Frankel, Bethany, 9
Frasier, 10, 11
Frasier dolphin, 157
Frasier, Shelly-Ann, 97
Freedom of the Seas, 134
Fremont Bridge, 293
Freshwater Center, 287
Freshwater fish, 188
Friedrich, Heike, 95
Frog, 176

G

Gaboon viper, 178
Gabriel, Peter, 48
Garnett, Kevin, 55
Garson, Greer, 16
Garvey, Steve, 88
Gatlin, Justin, 96
Geboers, Eric, 107
Geese in Flight, 279
Gehrig, Lou, 87, 88
Gentoo penguin, 163
Georgia, 255, 263
Georgia Dome, 228
Georgia Sports Hall of Fame, 255
German shepherd, 189
Germany, 102, 125, 241
Geysers, 257
Gharial, 183
Giant flying fox, 174
Giant sequoia, 198
Giant spider crab, 153
Giant squid, 154
Giant water lily, 200
Giant Wheel, 288
Gift, The, 34
Gifu Freshwater Aquarium, 287
Gill, Vince, 47
Giraffe, 169, 173
Glass squid, 154
Glee cast, 37
G-LYNX, 141
Gmail, 121
GNC, 223
Gobi Desert, 149
Golden Jubilee, 145
Golden retriever, 189
Golf, 72–76
Goliath frog, 180, 181
Goliath spider, 184

Gomez, Selena, 8
Google, 121, 122, 124
Gordon, Jeff, 105
Gorilla, 175
Gosselin, Kate, 9
Graf, Steffi, 90, 92
Grand Canyon National Park, 237
Gray whale, 160
Great blue heron, 165
Great Lakes Aquarium, 287
Great Sand Dunes, 251
Great Smoky Mountains, 237
Great white shark, 155, 156, 159
Greeley Stampede, 295
Green Monster, 138
Green, Maurice, 96
Greenland, 126, 152
Greenland shark, 155
Gretzky, Wayne, 111
Griffey, Jr., Ken, 77
Griffith Joyner, Florence, 97
Grizzly bear, 168
Gulf War, 206

H

Hagen, Walter, 75
Hailstones, 272
Haislett, Nicole, 95
Halas, George, 68
Half marathon, 259
Hamm, Mia, 100
Haneda International, 239
Hanks, Tom, 21, 26
Hargitay, Mariska, 7
Harmon, Mark, 6
Harry Potter, 25
Harry Potter and the Deathly Hallows, 23, 30
Harry Potter and the Half Blood Prince, 29
Hartack, Bill, 109
Hartness State Airport, 265
Hartsfield-Jackson Atlanta International, 239
Haslam, Leon, 108
Hassan, Ahmed, 101
Hassan, Hossam, 101
Hatcher, Teri, 7
Hawaii, 248, 256, 261
Hawk moth, 185

Hawk, Tony, 114, 115
Hayman Pool, 231
Heathrow Airport, 239
Heinrich Hertz Telescope, 256
Helicopters, 141
Hell Gate Bridge, 293
Hello, Dolly!, 49
Henderson, Ricky, 81
Henry, Thierry, 99
Hepburn, Katharine, 16
Hersheypark, 225
"Hey, Soul Sister," 36, 44
HHHR Tower, 227
Hill Street Blues, 10
Hinault, Bernard, 71
Hippopotamus, 169
Hiway 50 Drive In, 283
Hogan, Ben, 75
Holland Tunnel, 277
Holmes, Priest, 65
Honda Accord, 220
Hong Kong, 226
Hoosac Tunnel, 292
Hornet, 185
Horse races, 262
Hot air balloons, 276
Hotel suites, 211
Hotels, 211, 229
Hotmail, 121
Howe, Gordie, 111
HP, 129
Huet, Nicolas, 116
Huffman, Felicity, 7
Hugh Hefner Sky Villa, 211
Humboldt-Toiyabe National Forest, 247
Humpback whale, 161
Hurricane, 208
Hurricane Allen, 208
Hurricane Camille, 208
Hurricane Gilbert, 208
Hurricane Katrina, 205, 208
Hurricane Mitch, 208

I

"I Gotta Feeling," 40
Ice Age: Dawn of the Dinosaurs, 22
Iceland, 126
Icon Sheene, 217
Idaho, 247, 257, 282
Idlewood Park, 252
Illinois, 253, 258, 272, 288, 291

Independence of the Seas, 134
India, 127
Indian Ocean, 151
Indiana, 61, 259, 260, 273
Indurain, Miguel, 71
Inkster, Juli, 74
International Balloon Fiesta, 276
International Commerce Center, 230
Internet, 126, 127
Iowa, 260
iPhone, 212
Iron Man 2, 23
Islands, 152
Italy, 102, 131, 235

J

Jackson, Alan, 47
Jackson, Lauren, 57, 58
Jackson, Samuel L., 21
Jacoby, Mike, 116
James Clerk Maxwell Telescope, 256
James, LeBron, 53
Japan, 127, 131, 204, 241, 287
Japanese cedar, 198
Jarzoo Boardwalk, 275
Jay-Z, 39
Jets, 142
Jobe, Georges, 107
Johnson, Jimmie, 105
Johnson, Randy, 78, 85
Jones, Angus T., 8
Jones, Cobi, 101
Jordan, Michael, 53, 56
Joseph, Curtis, 112
Journal Pavilion, 270
Jumeirah Emirates Tower, 229
"Just Dance," 40

K

K2, 146
Kahal Kadosh Beth Elohim Synagogue, 284
Kaka, 99
Kalahari Desert, 149
Kalahari Resort, 268
Kangchenjunga, 146
Kansas, 253, 261, 272, 295

Kansas City, 261, 266
Kansas Sports Hall of Fame, 255
Kardashian, Kim, 9, 213
Kawasaki Ninja ZX-14, 140
Ke$ha, 35, 45
Keith, Toby, 42
Kelso Dunes, 251
Kentucky, 61, 262, 265, 288
Kentucky Derby, 262
Kerr, Cristie, 73, 74
KFC, 222
Kim, Song-Hee, 73
King cobra, 177
King penguin, 163
Kingda Ka, 132, 133
Kings of Leon, 41
Kitt Peak National Observatory, 248
Kiwi, 166
Kodiak bear, 168
Koenigsegg Agera, 216
Komodo dragon, 182
Kuchar, Matt, 72
Kuffman Stadium, 266

L

Labrador retriever, 189
Lady Antebellum, 34, 37, 45, 46
Lady Gaga, 35, 40, 43, 46, 48
Ladybug, 187
Lafayette, 246
Lake Chelan, 282
Lake Compounce, 252
Lake Huron, 148
Lake Michigan, 148
Lake Pend, 282
Lake Superior, 148, 282
Lake Tahoe, 282
Lake Victoria, 148
Lakemont Park, 252
Lakes, 148, 282
Lambeau, Curly, 68
Lamborghini Reventon, 216
Landry, Tom, 68
Las Vegas, 273
Lasek, Bucky, 114
Last Emperor, The, 15
Late Show with David Letterman, The, 11
Laurie, Hugh, 6
Laver, Rod, 93
Led Zeppelin, 38

Lee, Stan, 20
Lemmon's Petrified Wood Park, 286
Lemon shark, 159
Les Miserables, 50
Leslie, Lisa, 58
Lesser yellowleg, 164
Levi, Zachary, 213
Lewis, Rashard, 55
LG Electronics, 128
Lhotse, 146
Liberty of the Seas, 134
Lick Observatory, 248
Lightning, 254
Lil Wayne, 39
Lilly, Kristine, 100
Limbaugh, Rush, 14
Lincoln Tunnel, 277
Lituya Bay, 203
LIVESTRONG, 214
Lizard, 182
Lloro, 194
Lockheed SR-71 Blackbird, 143
Logano, Joey, 106
London, 228, 242
Long Logs Forest, 286
Longoria, Eva, 7, 213
Lord of the Rings, The, 25
Lord of the Rings: The Return of the King, The, 15, 24
Los Angeles, 266
Los Angeles Lakers, 52
Lottery, 274
Louisiana, 249, 254, 263, 269, 278
Louisiana Tech, 60
"Love the Way You Lie," 36, 45
"Low," 40
Lufthansa, 240
Lynn Auto Theater, 283

M

Macau, 130
Macchia Nera, 217
MacDonald, Andy, 114, 115
Madagascar, 152
Maddux, Greg, 85
Madonna, 43, 48
Magic Kingdom, 225, 234
Magnolia, 200
Maine, 264, 283, 290
Maine coon, 190

Makalu, 146
Mako shark, 158, 159
Malmo, 244
Malone, Karl, 56
Manchester United, 218
Manning, Eli, 69
Manning, Payton, 62, 69
Mansell, Nigel, 103
Mantle, Mickey, 82
Maple syrup, 290
Marabou stork, 162
Mardi Gras, 246
Marino, Dan, 62
Mario Kart, 120
Marlin, 158
Martin, Curtis, 63
Martinez, Pedro, 85
Mary Tyler Moore Show, The, 10
Maryland, 262, 265, 285
Mass Destruction, 136
Massachusetts, 264, 266, 277, 285, 292
Mauna Kea, 248, 256
Maybach Landaulet, 216
Mays, Willie, 77
McDonalds, 222
McGraw, Dr. Phil, 14
McGwire, Mark, 76, 219
Meloni, Chris, 6
Mentalist, The, 12
Merckx, Eddy, 71
Messi, Lionel, 99
Messier, Mark, 111
Metro AG, 221
Mexico, 238
Miami, 236
Miami Dolphins, 68, 70
Michigan, 267, 273, 282
Michigan Stadium, 232, 267
Microsoft Windows Mobile, 129
Middlesboro-Bell County Airport, 265
MiG-25R Foxbat B, 143
Migration, 187
Mille Fiori, 273
Miller Outdoor Theater, 270
Minnesota, 261, 268, 282, 287
Mirra, Dave, 115

Mississippi, 249, 254, 269, 278
Mississippi-Missouri River, 150
Mississippi Sports Hall of Fame, 255
Missouri, 249, 270, 288, 292, 294
Moffat Tunnel, 292
Monarch butterfly, 187
Mongolian gazelle, 172
Monk parakeet, 165
Monster trucks, 136
Montana, 271
Montenegro, 130
Montreal Canadiens, 110, 113
Moon, Warren, 62
Moose, 173
Morceli, Noureddine, 89
Moscow, 242, 243
Moss, Randy, 64
Motorcycles, 140, 217
Mount Baker, 191
Mount Everest, 146
Mount Rainer, 191
Mount Washington, 196
Mountain Dell Dam, 281
Mountains, 146
Movie theaters, 233
MTT Turbine SuperBike, 217
MTV, 48
Muny, 270
Murphy, Eddie, 21
Museum of Ancient Life, 289
Museums, 285, 289
Mushroom, 199
Musial, Stan, 79, 83
Mute swan, 162
MV-Augusta, 217
MV Augusta F4 1000 Tamburini, 140
MV Augusta F41100 CC, 140
My World 2.0, 34
Myers, Mike, 18

N

Nadal, Rafael, 91
Naismith, Dr. James, 219
National forests, 247
National parks, 237

Navratilova, Martina, 92
Navy Pier Ferris Wheel, 288
NCAA, 59, 60
NCIS, 12
NCIS: Los Angeles, 12
Nebraska, 272
Need You Now, 34, 44, 45
Nesterenko, Yuliya, 97
Nevada, 251, 268, 271, 273, 295
New England Patriots, 67, 70, 218
New Guinea, 152
New Hampshire, 274, 290
New Jersey, 274, 275, 293
New Mexico, 270, 276
New Orleans, 246
New River Gorge Bridge, 293
New Super Mario Bros, 118
New Waddell Dam, 281
New York, 248, 250, 252, 253, 262, 275, 277, 284, 285, 290, 291, 293
New York City, 226, 236, 242, 243
New York Giants, 67
New York Mets, 80
New York Rangers, 113
New York Yankees, 80, 84, 218
Newman, Paul, 17
Neyland Stadium, 267
Ngeny, Noah, 89
Nicholson, Jack, 17
Nickelodeon Universe, 268
Nicklaus, Jack, 75
Nile, 150
Nintendo DS, 119
Noah's Ark, 294
Noel, Chuck, 68
Nokia, 128
North Carolina, 61, 278
North Dakota, 279
Norway, 125, 126
"Nothin' on You," 44

O

O'Neal, Shaquille, 56
O'Neill, Susie, 95
O2, 228
Oakland, 266

Oasis of the Seas, 134
Ocean Dome, 231
Oceans of Fun, 294
Ochoa, Lorena, 74
Oh! Calcutta!, 50
Ohev Sholom Talmud Torah, 284
Ohio, 252, 260, 267, 280, 283, 288
Ohio Stadium, 267
Oil spill, 206
Oita Stadium, 228
Ojos del Salado, 147
Oklahoma, 273, 281
Oklahoma City, 207
Old Perpetual, 257
Olivier, Laurence, 17
Olympic National Park, 237
"OMG," 44
One America 500 Festival Mini Marathon, 259
One Capital City, 227
Opera House, 233
Orangutan, 175
Orca, 157, 161
Oregon dunes, 251
Oregon, 279, 282, 293
Orlando, 236
Orthleib Pool, 231
Ostrich, 166
Owens, Terrell, 64

P

P.F. Chang's Rock 'n' Roll Half Marathon, 259
Pacarana, 170
Pacific Ocean, 151
Pacino, Al, 17
Pagani Zonda C9, 216
Page Field, 265
Page, Geraldine, 16
Paisley, Brad, 47
Palms Casino & Resort, 211
Paradise Station, 191
Paris, 243
Parker, Sarah Jessica, 27
Parthenon at Mt. Olympus, 268
Patagonia, 149
Patagonian cavy, 170
Patridge, Audrina, 9
Pattinson, Robert, 18
Payton, Walter, 63
Peabody Essex Museum, 285

Peale Museum, 285
Peel P50, 137
Pellegrini, Federica, 95
Penguin, 163
Pennsylvania, 250, 252, 253, 260, 267, 274, 283, 289
Pensacola, 246
Pensacola Dam, 281
Pentagon, 291
Peppers, Julius, 69
Perentie, 182
Perry, Katy, 35, 36, 44
Perry, Tyler, 32
Persian, 190
Petrified wood, 286
Petronas Twin Towers, 230
Pets, 188
Pettersen, Suzann, 73
Petty, Richard, 104
PGA, 72
Phantom of the Opera, The, 50
Phelps, Michael, 94
Philadelphia Phillies, 80
Philippines, 203, 204
Phoenix Suns, 54
Pilgrim Hall, 285
Pink Floyd, 38
Pirates of the Caribbean: At World's End, 29
Pirates of the Caribbean: Dead Man's Chest, 23
Pittsburgh Steelers, 67
Pizza Hut, 222
Planes, 143
Player, Gary, 75
Plays, 50, 51
Poison dart frog, 176
Pokémon Diamond/Pearl, 120
Pokémon Heart Gold/Silver Soul, 120
Pokémon White/Black, 120
"Poker Face," 40
Polar bear, 168
Poll, Claudia, 95
Pondexter, Cappie, 57
Porcupine, 170
Porsche 911, 139
Portland, 244
Preakness, 262
President Wilson Hotel, 211

Presidential Suite, 211
Primates, 175
Producers, The, 49
Pronghorn antelope, 172
Prost, Alain, 103
PS3, 119
PSP, 119
Pujols, Albert, 83
Pumpkins, 253
Purple Rain, 33

Q
Q1, 227

R
R.E.M., 48
Radio City Music Hall, 233
Radio Shack, 223
Rafflesia, 200
Ragdoll, 190
Rainbow Forest, 286
Raj Palace, 211
Rampone, Christie, 100
Ratzenberger, John, 21
Rea, Jonathon, 108
Recovery, 34, 35, 41
Recycling, 209
Red knot, 164
Redd, Michael, 55
Reliant Astrodome, 228
Reno Rodeo, 295
Requiem shark, 156
Resolute, 192
Retailers, 221
Reticulated python, 177
REVA G-Wiz, 137
Reykjavík, 244
Rhinoceros, 173
Rhode Island, 284
Rice, 249
Rice, Jerry, 64
Rida, Flo, 40
Rides, 225, 234
Right whale, 160
RIM Blackberry, 129
Ringtones, 45
Ripken, Jr., Carl, 86, 88
Rivers, 150
Rivers, Philip, 69
Robert, Joel, 107
Roberts, Fireball, 106
Robertson Airport, 265

Rock 'n' Roll San Antonio Half Marathon, 259
Rock 'n' Roll Virginia Beach Half Marathon, 259
Rock python, 177
Rocky Mountain Dinosaur Research Center, 289
Rodeo of the Ozarks, 295
Rodeos, 295
Rodriguez, Alex, 82
Roller coasters, 132
Romania, 98
Ronaldo, Cristiano, 99
Roosevelt Lake Bridge, 293
Rose Tower, 229
Rose, Pete, 79, 86
Roy, Patrick, 112
Royal Penthouse Suite, 211
Royal Villa, 211
Rungrado May First Stadium, 232
Running, 259
Russell's viper, 179
Russia, 98, 204, 238
Ruth, Babe, 77, 81, 87, 219
Ryan, Nolan, 78
Ryugyong Hotel, 229

S
Saco Drive-in, 283
Sadovyi, Yevgeny, 94
Saguaro, 197
Sahara Desert, 149
Sailfish, 158
Saint Lucia, 126
Salt Lake Stadium, 232
Saltwater crocodile, 183
Sampras, Pete, 91, 93
Samsung, 128
San Alfonso Del Mar, 231
San Antonio Spurs, 52, 54
San Francisco 49ers, 67
Sand dunes, 251
Sand Mountain, 251
Sande, Earl, 109
Sanders, Barry, 63
Sandler, Adam, 18, 26
Saturday Night Fever, 33

Sawchuck, Terry, 112
Schlitterbahn Waterpark, 294
Schmidt, Mike, 83
Schumacher, Michael, 103
Scott, Everett, 88
Sculpture, 273, 279
Seabreeze Park, 252
Seacrest, Ryan, 14, 213
Search engines, 124
Seeds, 202
Senna, Ayrton, 103
Seoul, 243
700T, 135
7-Eleven, 223
Shanghai, 226, 242
Shanghai World Financial Center, 230
Shankweiler's Drive-in Theater, 283
Sharks, 156
Sheen, Charlie, 6
Shin, Jiyai, 73
Shoemaker, Bill, 109
Shopping, 123
Shrek 2, 22
Shrek the Third, 22
Shul of New York, 284
Shula, Don, 68
Shuster, Joe, 215
Siegel, Jerry, 215
Sikorsky S76C, 141
Sikorsky X-2, 141
Silver Bullet, 142
Silverstone, Alicia, 19
Six Flags Ferris Wheel, 288
Six Flags Great Adventure, 132, 225
Skowhegan State Fair, 264
Skyscrapers, 226
Sloth bear, 168
Smart Car, 137
Smart phones, 129, 212
SMART-1, 142
"Smile," 45
Smith, Emmitt, 63–65
Smith, Katie, 58
Smith, Margaret Court, 92
Smith, Tangela, 58
Smith, Will, 18
Smithsonian Museum of Natural History, 289

Snakes, 177
Snowfall, 191
Sociable weaver, 165
Soda Springs, 257
Sorenstam, Annika, 74
Sosa, Sammy, 76
South Carolina, 254, 262, 263, 276, 284, 285
South Dakota, 272, 279, 286
South Korea, 241
South Pacific, 49
South Pole, 196
Southwest Airlines, 240
Spain, 235
Speak Now, 34
Speaker, Tris, 79
Spears, Britney, 43
Sperm whale, 160, 161
Sphynx, 190
Spider, 184
Spider-Man 3, 23, 29
Spielberg, Steven, 32
Spirit of America, 138
Sports cars, 216
Sports franchises, 218
Sports halls of fame, 255
Sports memorabilia, 219
Spring Awakening, 49
Springsteen, Bruce, 42
Sprouse, Cole, 8
Sprouse, Dylan, 8
St. Louis Cardinals, 84
Stadiums, 232, 267
Stanford, 60
Stankowski, Paul, 72
Star Dune, 251
Star Wars, 25
Starlight Theater, 270
Steel Dragon 2000, 132, 133
Stern, Howard, 14
Stewart, Jackie, 103
Stewart, Kristen, 19
Stiller, Ben, 26
Stover, Matt, 66
Strait, George, 47
Streep, Meryl, 16
Stricker, Steve, 72
Stull Observatory, 248
Suarez, Claudio, 101
Submillimeter wavelength telescope, 256
Subway, 222

Subway systems, 242
Sunflower, 200
Sunset Drive-in, 283
Super Bowl, 67
Super Smash Bros. Brawl, 120
Superman, 215
Superman Returns, 29
Superman: The Escape, 132
Survivor: Heroes vs. Villains, 13
Suzuki GSX1300R Hayabusa, 140
Swainson's hawk, 164
Sweden, 126, 275
Sweet potatoes, 278
Swift, Taylor, 34, 37, 41
Swimming pools, 231
Switzerland, 211

T

Taipan, 179
Taipei 101, 230
Tangled, 28
Tango T600, 137
Taurasi, Diana, 57
Ted Williams Tunnel, 277
Tejada, Miguel, 88
Telescopes, 248
Television, 131
Temples, 284
Tennessee, 60, 259, 267, 283, 287
Tennessee Aquarium, 287
Tesco, 221
Texas, 250, 261, 263, 269–271, 276, 288, 294
Texas Star, 288
Theaters, 270
Thimble Shoal Tunnel, 277
Thomas, Donald, 106
Thompson, Tina, 58
Thorpe, Ian, 94
Three County Fair, 264
Thrust 2, 138
Thrust SSC, 138
Thurman, Uma, 19
Tiger shark, 155, 156, 159
Tipas, 147
Titanic, 15, 24, 33
Tokyo, 226, 242, 243
Tokyo Disneyland, 234

Tokyo DisneySea, 234
Tomlinson, LaDainian, 64, 65
Tongass National Forest, 247
Tonto National Forest, 247
Tony Awards, 50
Top Thrill Dragster, 132, 133
Tornado, 207
Toronto Maple Leafs, 110, 113
Tourism, 235, 236
Touro Synagogue, 284
Tower of Terror, 132
Towers, 229, 230
Toy Story 3, 22, 28, 31
Toyota Camry, 220
Toyota Corolla, 220
Tracy, Spencer, 17
Train, 36, 44
Trains, 135, 292
Transformers: Revenge of the Fallen, 30
Tree, 198
Trek Madone, 214
Trump International Hotel & Tower, 258
Trumpeter swan, 162
Tsunami, 203
Tunnels, 277, 292
Turkey, 131
Tweets, 213
Twilight Saga: Eclipse, The, 30, 31
Twilight Saga: New Moon, The, 23, 30, 31
Twins Day Festival, 280
Twins Weekend, 280
Twitchange, 213
Two and a Half Men, 6, 12
Ty Warner Penthouse, 211

U

U2, 46
UCLA, 61
Ukraine, 98
Uncle Kracker, 45
United Airlines, 240
United Arab Emirates, 130, 133
United Kingdom, 125, 131, 287

United States, 98, 125, 127, 131, 235, 238, 241
University of Connecticut, 59
University of Michigan, 267
Up, 28
Urban, Keith, 42
Uruguay, 102
Usher, 44
Utah, 271, 281, 289

V

V-22 Osprey, 141
Van den Hoogenband, Pieter, 94
Vancouver, 244
Vermont, 264, 265, 290
Video games, 118–120
Virginia, 259, 277, 291
Virginia Sports Hall of Fame, 255
Viva La Vida, 41
Volcanoes, 147

W

Wagner, Honus, 219
Wahoo, 158
WALL-E, 28
Wal-Mart, 221
Walmart.com, 123
Waltrip, Darrell, 105
Washington Redskins, 218
Washington, 282, 292
Washington, DC, 289
Water monitor, 182
Water parks, 294
Weather, 261
Websites, 122–125
Webb, Karrie, 74
Welker, Frank, 21
Wescott, Seth, 116
West Indian butterfly, 185
West Side Story, 15
West Virginia, 293
West Wing, The, 11
West, Jerry, 53
West, Kanye, 42
Whale shark, 155
White rhinoceros, 169
White, Dana, 213
White, Shaun, 115
White-beaked dolphin, 157

White-rumped sandpiper, 164
Whooper swan, 162
Wii, 119
Wii Fit Plus, 118
Wii Sports Resort, 118
Wii Sports, 118
Williams, Serena, 89
Williams, Venus, 89
Willis Tower, 258, 291
Wills-Moody, Helen, 92
Wilson, Dean, 72
Wind, 196, 261
Windows Live, 121
Winfrey, Oprah, 14
Wisconsin, 268, 270, 282, 290, 294
Wisconsin Dells, 294
Witherspoon, Reese, 27
Wolves, 171
Woods, Tiger, 75
Woodstock Fair, 264
World Championship Punkin Chunkin, 253
Wrigley Field, 266
Wyoming, 261, 289, 295

X

X-15, 143
X-2, 143
X360, 119
X-43A, 143

Y

Yahoo! Mail, 121, 122
Yangtze River, 205
Yangtze-Kiang, 150
Yarborough, Cale, 105
Yastrzemski, Carl, 86
Yellow-eyed penguin, 163
Yellowstone National Park, 237
Yenisei Angara, 150
YMCA, 219
Yorkshire terrier, 189
Yosemite National Park, 237
Young Money, 45
YouTube, 122

Z

ZTE, 128
Zuckerberg, Mark, 122

photo credits

Northcott/Corbis; 177: Joe McDonald/Corbis; 178: Joe McDonald/Corbis; 179: Joe McDonald/Corbis; 180: HO/Reuters/Corbis; 181: Andrew Murray/Nature Picture Library; 182: Driverjcs/Dreamstime.com; 183: Franco Banfi/Photo Library; 184: Pete Oxford/Minden; 185: Malcolm Schuyl/FLPA/Photolibrary; 186: Ted Levin/Animals Animals; 187: Dreamstime; 188: Dompr/Dreamstime; 189: Nagel Photography/Shutterstock; 190: Linn Currie/Shutterstock; 191: Dean Pennala/Shutterstock; 192: Staffan Widstrand/Corbis; 193: Media Bakery; 194: Juan Manuel Barreto/AP Photo; 195: David Garry/Dreamstime; 196: Suzanne Long/Alamy; 197: Beisea/Dreamstime; 198: William Perry/Dreamstime; 199: George McCarthy/Corbis; 200: Kira Kaplinski/Dreamstime; 201: Michael Boys/Corbis; 202: Wolfgang Kaehler/Corbis; 203: Lloyd Cluff/Corbis; 204: Corbis; 205: Phil Coale/AP Photo; 206: Roberto Borea/AP Photo; 207: Reuters/Corbis; 208: Jack Thornell/AP Photo; 209: Davo Blair/Alamy.

Money:
210: Getty Images; Money icon: Svlumagraphica/Dreamstime.com; 211: President Wilson Hotel, Geneva; 212: Getty Images; 214: Bas Czerwinski/AP Photo; 215: Timothy A. Clary/AFP/Getty Images; 216: Laurent Cipriani/AP Photo; 217: ECOSSE Moto Works; 218: Andrew Yates/AFP/Getty Images; 219: Bebeto Matthews/AP Photo; 220: 2009 Ford Motor Company; 221: Bruce Glassman; 222: Imaginechina via AP Images; 223: Dale de la Rey/Bloomberg via Getty Images.

Human-made:
224: Media Bakery; Human-made icon: Joel Calheiros/Dreamstime.com; 225: Travis Schaeffer/Dreamstime.com; 226: Daumiu/Shutterstock; 227: Neale Cousland/Shutterstock; 228: Sergio Pitamitz/Corbis; 229: Rotana Hotel; 230: Kamran Jebreili/AP Photo; 231: Focus/Alamy; 232: Korean Central News Agency via Korea News Service/AP Photo; 233: © Paul Hawthorne/Getty Images; 235: Bruce Robbins/Dreamstime.com; 236: Ramon Grosso Dolarea/Shutterstock; 237: Paul Lemke/Dreamstime.com; 238: Rainer Grosskopf/Getty Images; 239: Barry Williams/Getty Images; 240: Ivan Cholakov Gostock-dot-net/Shutterstock; 241: Imaginechina/AP Images; 242: Jimmy Lopes/Dreamstime.com; 243: Galina Barskaya/People Dreamstime.com; 244: Steve Allen/Getty Images.

US:
245: Lake Compounce; US icon: Lesapi/Dreamstime.com; 246: William Manning/Corbis; 247: Mark A. Johnson/Corbis; 248: Ron Adcock/Dreamstime.com; 249: Belliot/Dreamstime.com; 250: Jed Jacobsohn/Getty Images; 251: Tony Sweet/Media Bakery; 253: Luc Viatour/Wikipedia; 254: Jeff Kinsey/Dreamstime.com; 255: Georgia Sports Hall of Fame; 256: Roger Ressmeyer/Corbis; 257: www.sodaspringsid.com; 258: Doris De Witt/Getty Images; 259: Ed Bock/Corbis; 260: Kim Pin Tan/Dreamstime.com; 261: Scott T. Smith/Corbis; 262: AP Photo; 263: Media Bakery; 264: Layne Kennedy/Corbis; 265: College Park Aviation Museum; 266: Kevin Fleming/Corbis; 267: Andrew Horne/Wikipedia; 268: Bill Ross/Corbis; 269: Philip Gould/Corbis; 270: James A. Finley/AP Photo; 271: Sekernas/Dreamstime.com; 272: Steve Swazo/AP Photo; 273: David Samuel Robbins/Corbis; 274: zentilia/

Shutterstock; 275: Bob Krist/Corbis; 276: Steve Estvanik/Shutterstock; 277: John Munson/Star Ledger/Corbis; 278: Monkey Business Images/Dreamstime.com; 279: Gary Greff; 280: Evan Hurd/Corbis; 281: John Elk III/Getty Images; 282: Bruce Shippee/Dreamstime.com; 283: Darlene Bordwell; 284: Bob Krist/Corbis; 285: Yalonda M. James/Post and Courier/AP Photo; 286: Tom Bean/Corbis; 287: Tennessee Aquarium; 288: Richard Cummins/Corbis; 289: Leon7/Wikipedia; 290: Anikasalsera/Dreamstime.com; 291: Corbis; 292: George White Location Photography; 293: Brendan Reals/Shutterstock; 294: Amy Muller/Noah's Ark; 295: Michael Smith/The Wyoming Tribune Eagle/AP Photo.

Bonus Section:
305 top: Jae C. Hong/AP Photo; 305 bottom left: Patrik Stollarz/AFP/Getty Images; 305 bottom right: Splash News and Pictures/Newscom; 306 left: Bob D'Amico/Disney Channel via Getty Images; 306 right: Adam Taylor/ABC via Getty Images; 307 top: Hanna Barbera/The Kobal Collection; 307 bottom: Mike Weaver/ABC via Getty Images; 308: Disney Pixar/Newscom; 309 left: Walt Disney Pictures/Album/Newscom; 309 right: Jeff Kravitz/FilmMagic/Getty Images; 310 bottom: Jason DeCrow/AP Photo; 311: Wade Payne/AP Photo; 312: HO/AFP/Getty Images/Newscom; 313 top: Lionel Cironneau/AP Photo; 313 bottom: Julie Robertson/Getty Images; 315 left: Frank Franklin II/AP Photo; 315 right: Duomo/Corbis; 316 bottom: NASA; 317 bottom: NASA.

BONUS SECTION

A Mind-blasting Collection of Weird and Wacky Facts

television ● movies ● music
travel ● sports ● space

what's in a name?

Cole and Dylan Sprouse—stars of Nickelodeon's *The Suite Life on Deck*— were given celebrity names before they themselves were famous. Cole is named after the famous musician Nat King Cole, and Dylan is named after the well-known poet Dylan Thomas. Cole is just 15 minutes younger than Dylan and has a mole on his cheek that helps fans tell them apart.

styling up the stars

Dancing with the Stars contestants and professional dancers use more than 100 different costumes each month. The designers have six days to create each outfit, and they use more than 200,000 rhinestones each season. Since costumes are used only once, many are sold online for up to $5,000.

television

stone age celebration

On September 30, 2010, *The Flintstones* celebrated its 50th anniversary. The Hanna-Barbera classic was originally a prime-time show which went on to launch seven spin-offs and five made-for-TV movies. *The Flintstones* was the first cartoon to have celebrities lend their voices as guest stars on a weekly basis, and some of the best known included Dick Clark, Tony Curtis, and Ann-Margret.

safety first!

Contestants competing on the crazy obstacles of *Wipeout* may seem doomed for disaster, but there is actually an extensive safety check in place. First, the creators spend about $200,000 in padding each season, which coats everything in 6 to 24 inches (15 to 61 cm) of foam. There is also a Black and Blue Crew—made up of several men and women of different ages and sizes—who test everything from impact to water temperature.

tv time overload

The average American child sees more than 20,000 30-second commercials each year. That's about 167 hours, or almost 7 straight days of advertisements. Each child also watches a total of 62 days of television each year. About half of all kids ages 6 to 17 have a TV in their bedroom, and 66 percent watch TV while eating dinner.

sweet deal

The three cookie-selling orphans in *Despicable Me* need to carry a calculator. According to Margo's clipboard of cookie prices, each box is $6. The evil Vector orders 4 Minty Mints, 15 Coconutties, 2 Toffee Totes, and 2 Caramel Clumps. His bill should have been $138, but the girls only ask him for $52.

attention to detail

During the planning stages, *Toy Story 3* creators produced 92,854 storyboards laying out the film; half of these were given to editorial for different script ideas. In the end, 302 characters were created for the film. Woody and Buzz each have more than 200 points of movement on their faces to show expression, and Lotso the bear has more than 3.4 million individual hairs covering his body.

vying for the vampire's volvo

Before the release of *The Twilight Saga: Eclipse,* Volvo featured an online game in which competitors had to navigate a maze of the movie's setting—Forks, Washington—in order to reach Bella's graduation party at the Cullen house. The player who reached the party in the shortest number of turns won the same car Edward drives in the movie—a shiny silver Volvo XC60.

digital double

Armie Hammer played twins Cameron and Tyler Winklevoss in *The Social Network* after an actual set of twin actors could not be found. Another actor—Josh Pence—physically acted as one of the brothers with Hammer, but then Pence's face was digitally replaced with Hammer's. The two actors even took classes to mirror each other's movements.

pirate peril

Pirates of the Caribbean: On Stranger Tides was filmed on location in Hawaii, and some of the scenes were shot in the thick coconut groves at the once-famous Coco Palms Hotel in Wailua. Before filming could begin, however, all 773 palm trees had to be harvested so that no falling coconuts could crack one of the cast or crew in the head during production.

shout with glee

In October 2010, the cast of *Glee* surpassed music legends The Beatles for most appearances on the Billboard charts by a non-solo act. With 75 hits on the Hot 100 chart, they topped The Beatles' record by 4. The Beatles' songs hit the charts between 1964 and 1996, but it took the *Glee* cast just one and a half years to top them. The songs that put them over the top were recorded for the Britney Spears episode.

"not afraid" of success

Eminem became the first artist to have the bestselling album of the year twice—first with *The Eminem Show* in 2002, and recently with *Recovery* in 2010. Because he had such a successful year, Eminem became the seventh bestselling artist in Nielsen history, and the fourth most-downloaded artist of all time.

raking in the digital dollars

In 2010, about 46 percent of all music purchases were digital. That totaled more than 1.17 billion songs sold that year. About 2.8 million songs were purchased the week ending December 26, making it the busiest week of 2010. Digital music sales have grown by more than 1,000 percent since 2004.

lucky thirteen

Lady Gaga became the most nominated artist in the history of the MTV Video Music Awards when she received 13 nominations in 2010. She went on to win 8 awards—Video of the Year, Best Pop Video, Best Female Video, Best Collaboration, Best Dance Music Video, Best Choreography, Best Direction, and Best Editing.

swift success

Each of the 14 tracks from Taylor Swift's album *Speak Now* hit the Hot 100 charts. She is the only artist to accomplish this feat. Swift also holds the record for the most top-ten debuts on the Hot 100 charts. The album debuted at number 1 on the Billboard 200 chart in October 2010 and sold more than 1.04 million copies.

underwater art

The Cancun Underwater Museum, located in Mexico's Cancun Marine Park, features 400 life-sized sculptures made of clay spread over 1,600 square feet (150 sq m) of ocean bottom. Although they are a popular attraction for scuba divers, the actual reason for this museum is to create an artificial reef for local marine life. The nearby natural reefs were damaged by hurricanes over the years.

no bones about it

The Dog Bark Park Inn is the only guesthouse located inside a giant wooden beagle. Located in Cottonwood, Idaho, this unique lodge has guests enter though a balcony on the second floor into the main residence. Guests can go up another floor, into the dog's head, for additional sleeping space. There is also a cozy alcove located in the beagle's muzzle.

mile-high meals

Dinner in the Sky offers diners the opportunity to eat gourmet food while suspended by a giant crane 150 feet (46 m) in the air! The cost for the high-rise meal is $6,500 for 22 people. Meals can last up to eight hours, but guests may want to skip that extra glass of water because there are no bathrooms! The first Dinner in the Sky opened in Brussels in 2006, and the culinary cranes are now in 15 cities, including Barcelona, Spain; Budapest, Hungary; and Toronto, Canada. Each evening's cuisine and location within the city can be chosen by the party host, as long as a land permit is available and there is room for the crane.

a room with a view

The Marmara Antalya is a luxury hotel in Turkey, set on the Falez Hills by the Mediterranean Sea. Its Revolving Loft building is the only spinning hotel in the world and offers guests 24 club rooms. The hotel rotates 2 to 24 times each day, giving guests spectacular 360-degree views of the surrounding landscape. For guests who prefer to remain in one place, the hotel also offers traditional rooms.

sticky situation

Behind the famed Pike Place Market in Seattle, Washington, stands a 50-foot-long (15 m) brick wall covered with millions of pieces of used chewing gum, which attracts tourists from across the country. Some areas of the wall are a few inches thick with gum in multiple colors. TripAdvisor recently rated that wall as one of the germiest attractions in the world.

x-tremely popular

Winter X Game attendance soared in 2011, with more than 114,200 fans turning out to see their favorite athletes compete in Aspen, Colorado—a 40 percent increase from 2010. The X Games Facebook page picked up 170,000 new fans and had more than 43 million views. ESPN also exchanged about 65,000 text messages with fans. Viewers were able to get quick updates on top athletes, including Shaun White, Kelly Clark, and Tucker Hibbert.

omniscient octopus

A German octopus named Paul became an international celebrity during the 2010 FIFA World Cup when he successfully predicted all seven of Germany's matches, as well as the cup's final match. To predict the outcome of an upcoming match, Paul was given two boxes of food, each with a flag of one of the teams. Whichever box he chose to eat out of was his winning pick.

goal-den scores

The highest-scoring hockey game in history took place during the 1998 Asia-Oceania Championship when South Korea beat Thailand with a score of 92–0. A 2008 European Olympic prequalifying match was the venue for the highest-scoring women's game. Slovakia beat Bulgaria with a score of 82–0. Slovakia averaged 1 goal every 44 seconds and made a total of 130 shots on goal.

this one really is a long shot (twice!)

Jack Nicklaus sank the longest putt in PGA history when he made a shot from 110 feet (33.5 m) away at the 1964 Tournament of Champions. More recently, Nick Price also sunk one from 110 feet (33.5 m) out in the 1992 PGA.

age is just a number

Major League Baseball players can succeed at any age. The oldest player to ever hit a home run is Julio Franco, who hit one at age 48 years and 245 days on May 4, 2007, while playing for the New York Mets. The youngest player to hit a home run is Tommy Brown—a Brooklyn Dodger who hit one out of the park at the age of 17 years and 257 days on August 20, 1945.

out-of-this-world price tag

For would-be astronauts who don't want to commit to NASA training, Virgin Galactic offers a chance to launch into space—for $200,000. A $20,000 deposit is needed to make a reservation, and a few hundred people have already signed on. This includes a three-day training course, and seminars with space enthusiast and company founder Richard Branson. Date of travel cannot be confirmed until Virgin is sure the journey is safe for all passengers.

galactic junk pile

Scientists better start cleaning up after themselves—there are more than 8,000 artificial objects floating above the Earth. About 2,500 of these are satellites, but the rest is known as space junk. This includes broken or nonfunctioning items such as rocket bodies or hatch covers. Gravity will eventually pull these pieces back to Earth, and NASA estimates that about one piece drops down each day.

they don't call it super for nothing

A supernova occurs when a gigantic star runs out of fuel and explodes. In 2006, scientists observed a supernova that was 100 times bigger than any they had ever seen. In just two months, the supernova released more radiation than the sun will in its 10-billion-year lifetime. The supernova, called SN 2006gy, is located 240 million light-years from Earth.

voting on venus?

Texas is the only state that lets its citizens vote from space. Astronaut David Wolf became the first person to do so when he cast his absentee ballot by e-mail for the mayor of Houston from the Russian space station Mir in 1997. Before this law was changed, absentee ballots had to be processed by the US mail. The change was made only for Texas, since most astronauts live there.

Read for the World Record!

KIDS ANSWERED THE CHALLENGE!

Kids from every state and around the world participated in the Scholastic Summer Challenge and Read for the World Record to set a record for summer reading!

Read for the World Record united students in an attempt to achieve a world record by reading for as many minutes as possible between April 27 and August 31, 2011.

CHECK OUT THESE COOL FACTS:

STATES WITH THE MOST MINUTES READ:

1. Florida
2. California
3. Alabama
4. Texas
5. North Carolina
6. Illinois
7. New York
8. Ohio
9. Georgia
10. New Jersey
11. Minnesota
12. Pennsylvania
13. Colorado
14. Michigan
15. Maryland
16. Massachusetts
17. Wisconsin
18. South Carolina
19. Indiana
20. Virginia

STATES WITH THE MOST MINUTES

Did your state make the top 20?

STUDENTS FROM AROUND THE WORLD PARTICIPATED!

Two international schools read enough minutes to rank in the top 100 worldwide: Our Lady of Mercy School in Rio de Janeiro, Brazil, and St. David's Primary School in St. David's, Bermuda. Schools from 20 other countries also added minutes to the world record, including:

Canada
China
Colombia
Dubai
Finland
France
India
Italy
Germany
Honduras
Japan
New Zealand
Oman
Saudi Arabia
Singapore
United Kingdom

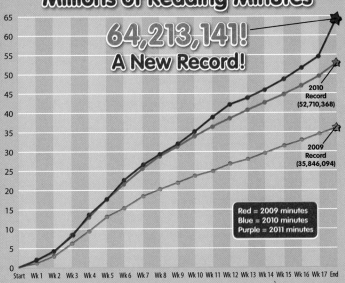

Millions of Reading Minutes

64,213,141!
A New Record!

2010 Record (52,710,368)

2009 Record (35,846,094)

Red = 2009 minutes
Blue = 2010 minutes
Purple = 2011 minutes

| 65 | 60 | 55 | 50 | 45 | 40 | 35 | 30 | 25 | 20 | 15 | 10 | 5 | 0 |

Start Wk 1 Wk 2 Wk 3 Wk 4 Wk 5 Wk 6 Wk 7 Wk 8 Wk 9 Wk 10 Wk 11 Wk 12 Wk 13 Wk 14 Wk 15 Wk 16 Wk 17 End

CONGRATULATIONS TO EVERYONE WHO HELPED SET THE RECORD!

Summer is Reading season

Total minutes read from
April 27 to August 31, 2011:

64,213,141

Total number of participating schools:

4,193

Total number of students:

101,361

Members of Brooksville Elementary School with their minutes.

THE TOP SUMMER READING SCHOOL!

Top honor in the 2011 Scholastic Summer Challenge goes to **Brooksville Elementary School** in Brooksville, FL, with **3,176,409** minutes logged toward Read for the World Record!

THE BEST OF THE REST WITH THE MOST READING MINUTES!

These schools all logged more than 500,000 minutes toward setting the new world record!

School	Location	Minutes
Beacon Cove Intermediate School	Jupiter, FL	2,464,096
St. Isidore School	Danville, CA	2,075,131
St. Gregory Cathedral School	Tyler, TX	1,553,670
Paine Intermediate School	Trussville, AL	1,449,044
Highland Elementary School	Sylvania, OH	1,362,203
Paine Primary School	Trussville, AL	956,355
Liberty Park Elementary School	Greenacres, FL	885,872
Broadview Elementary School	North Lauderdale, FL	779,732
Pleasant Grove Elementary School	Inverness, FL	727,481
Union Elementary School	Temple, GA	706,766
Osseo Area Schools Kidstop Summer Program	Maple Grove, MN	659,006
Enders-Salk Elementary School	Schaumburg, IL	625,193
Walker Elementary School	Chuluota, FL	623,075
J. Harold Van Zant Elementary School	Marlton, NJ	607,437
Bright Horizons	Charlotte, NC	591,796
Westdale Elementary School	Northlake, IL	586,742
Village Elementary School	Hilton, NY	566,098
Westview Middle School	Longmont, CO	563,235
Heritage Elementary School	Greenacres, FL	523,835
Matthews Elementary School	Matthews, NC	516,533

National Record

This Is To Certify That

SCHOLASTIC MALAYSIA

is listed in

THE MALAYSIA BOOK OF RECORDS

MOST NUMBER OF CHILDREN READING STORYBOOKS IN SCHOOLS IN A DAY

Total : 413, 595 children

Date : November 8, 2010

Co-organizer : Ministry of Education Malaysia

DATUK DANNY OOI *PJN*
Founder

This certificate was issued on **December 28, 2010**